Praise

Rock the Boat

"During Danelle's 30-plus years in the US Navy, she was recognized for her leadership, won numerous awards, and retired as an admiral responsible for the navy's cybersecurity policy. Danelle gives very specific advice for dealing with all kinds of organizational, management, and personal issues applicable for leaders across corporate America. I very much urge you to read this book . . . it will provide valuable teaching lessons no matter what profession you are in."

—**MARK AIN,** founder and former CEO of Kronos, profit and not-for-profit board member

"*Rock the Boat* is a great illustration of how our follies and foibles alongside our achievements weave the fabric of a successful career. It provides real, relatable, and useful tools for improved communication and self-awareness applicable to any industry. It gives you fun and practical lessons in leadership."

—**ROBERT TAVARES,** board member, KVH Industries, advisor for private equity, former president and CEO of API Technologies

"*Rock the Boat* provides an entire ocean of insights for individual contributors, mid-level managers, and senior executives. Ms. Barrett presents her unique leadership concepts with memorable humor and candor. Her foundational principles are easy to grasp and readily applied to challenges and opportunities in all business settings. If you want to lead change, 'Rock the Boat.'"

—**TINA SWALLOW,** sales director, McAfee

"This book is gold! It's rich in all the things that matter if you want to lead with integrity, humility, compassion, and humor. Former Rear Admiral Danelle Barrett nailed the most essential elements of leadership and mentorship. As I was reading, I was encouraged to adjust my own leadership style. This should be a staple in any leadership kitbag. Pull it out again and again to check your own leadership compass. I did!"

—**LIEUTENANT GENERAL LORI REYNOLDS,**
US Marine Corps

"Danelle's insightful approach to meaningful leadership transcends the scope of her years in the navy. I work in a creative industry and absolutely recognize the importance of what she has laid out in an incredibly digestible way. Her approach is one that understands the necessity of connecting with one another and leaning into different perspectives. Her guidance is precise and offers countless real-life applications that illustrate the core pillars of leadership. I think anyone stands to benefit from her expertise on fostering the best mentor/mentee relationship possible and achieving effective communication."

—**FRANKIE SHAW,** motion picture and
television director, writer, producer, and actor

"Former Rear Admiral Barrett distills plenty of navy wisdom in this highly readable and very practical guide to deckplate leadership. Of particular note are her thoughts on mentorship, a key practical skill set at the heart of servant leadership. A must-read for aspiring leaders from the world of business to the bridge of navy ships!"

—**ADMIRAL JIM STAVRIDIS,** former supreme
allied commander at NATO and author of
Sailing True North: Ten Admirals and the Voyage of Character

"A remarkable, down-to-earth primer for human leadership in the troubled times of the fantasyland of the 'tech-driven algorithm' world of the twenty-first century that will enable the human factor (reader) to survive and most importantly *thrive!*"

—**MB DILLON**, MD, founder, Green Crescent Health Insurance Company, Abu Dhabi, UAE

"Former Rear Admiral Danelle Barrett is the admiral other admirals aspire to. Not only did this book make me piss my pants I was laughing so hard and cry a river of tears because it compelled me to reflect on the increasing value of selfless sacrifice and servant leadership in our nation so full of incivility and misplaced hubris, but it made me consider my own failings as a leader (I didn't know I had so many). Each chapter is filled with wisdom; every sea story is rich with insight and learnable lessons that are knowable because they are familiar but oft forgotten. The whole damn thing is a treasure chest filled to the brim with uncommon sense. I've had the great honor to know and work with Danelle for almost two decades; she is a sailor's sailor and an officer of exemplary character. What's better, she knows operations, warfighting, and leadership. She raises everybody's game on the path to mission success. What's best is she does this with grace, humor, and commanding knowledge. This book is a great case study on succeeding as a leader in any structured, hide-bound, traditional hierarchy (not just the United States Navy) using minimum controls to achieve maximum outcomes."

—**TIMOTHY J. WHITE**, vice admiral (ret.), US Navy

"Irreverent yet mission-focused, Danelle Barrett is clearly a force of nature, and her book is no different. There's much to learn here about leadership when the pressure is on your team and the clock is ticking. She has taken some older maxims on managing people and breathed new life into them with insightful, practical ideas on leadership."

—GENE PRICE, member of the law firm
Frost, Brown, and Todd LLC

ROCK the
BOAT

Embrace Change,
Encourage Innovation,
and Be a Successful Leader

ROCK the
BOAT

DANELLE BARRETT

GREENLEAF
BOOK GROUP PRESS

Published by Greenleaf Book Group Press
Austin, Texas
www.gbgpress.com

Distributed by Greenleaf Book Group

For ordering information or special discounts for bulk purchases, please contact Greenleaf Book Group at PO Box 91869, Austin, TX 78709, 512.891.6100.

Design and composition by Greenleaf Book Group and Teresa Muniz
Cover design by Greenleaf Book Group and Teresa Muniz
Cover image used under license from @Shutterstock/Yeryomina Anastassiya,
Vector graphics used in the interior under license from
@the Noun Project/Diana Militano, @the Noun Project/Alena Artemova
Dance photography taken by Joseph Lyman featuring dancers including
Hayley-Ann Vasco and Tyveze Littlejohn
All other photography taken by Hayley-Ann Vasco

Publisher's Cataloging-in-Publication data is available.

Print ISBN: 978-1-62634-852-3

eBook ISBN: 978-1-62634-853-0

Part of the Tree Neutral® program, which offsets the number of trees consumed in the production and printing of this book by taking proactive steps, such as planting trees in direct proportion to the number of trees used: www.treeneutral.com

TreeNeutral

Printed in the United States of America on acid-free paper

21 22 23 24 25 26   10 9 8 7 6 5 4 3 2 1

First Edition

For Hayley-Ann and Gildardo Vasco, my hearts;
Mary and Pat Hays and Bob Barrett, my parents;
Admiral Bill "Fox" Fallon, my lifelong mentor;
and Theresa Tokarczyk McDonnell, my lifelong friend

CONTENTS

PREFACE

I recently transitioned from the US Navy back to civilian life after more than thirty years on active duty where I held many key leadership positions. I retired as a rear admiral specializing in communications, information technology, and cyber offensive and defensive operations. I wanted to write this book to share my first-hand experience serving in some of the toughest leadership positions across the nation.

Over my years in the service, I mentored hundreds of diverse people—both in and out of the military—and have spoken to hundreds of audiences, so I have the breadth and depth of direct experience to draw on for the lessons in this book. The advice in *Rock the Boat* transcends industries and is applicable in any leadership or management position, and I have included many of the most-requested topics of conversation from my mentees and conference attendees.

Even better, if you're tired of reading complicated leadership books, *Rock the Boat* gives leadership lessons and advice in plain, simple language supported by humorous, touching, and practical storytelling. It will also challenge you to find your "three positives" in any situation. I imagined this book as a conversation with your mentor over a cup of coffee, during which real, actionable guidance and recommendations for growth are discussed.

Stories I've heard and experienced throughout my career back up the lessons. You'll remember those touching, funny, serious, and relatable tales long after you've put the book down and acted on its recommendations. I hope that you come away with the feeling of enjoyable learning and practical, no-nonsense actions you can take to become a better leader and mentor.

You will also come away with creative approaches to handling tough leadership and mentoring challenges in an increasingly complex world where solutions and the vision needed for the future can feel overwhelming at times. *Rock the Boat* provides the simple, concise leadership and mentoring advice to develop change leaders who can make a better future for their organizations and those they mentor.

This book will empower you to be a great change leader and mentor with simple but important concepts, enabling you to develop other strong change leaders and mentors. In real-life situations, exceptional leadership isn't rocket science if you just focus on what matters most.

In fact, it's so easy a monkey could do it.

INTRODUCTION

L eadership, unlike management, is not science and numbers. It
is about people. It is intrinsic and learned behaviors that people use to inspire others to follow and exceed expectations while
achieving common objectives. Through innate ability and experience, everyone develops their own unique style as a leader. That
style is heavily influenced by both the good and bad behaviors they
have observed in other leaders over the years but remains unique
to each individual. Those who stand out are able to translate their
vision into reality by the way they communicate, connect, and collaborate with others to generate excitement about that vision and
see their role in achieving it. A leader's courage, tenacity, and ability
to not be deterred by cynics or obstacles motivate others to follow in
their footsteps.

We are faced today with the unprecedented, accelerating, and
exponential pace of technological advancement, which is fundamentally revolutionizing whole segments of society. Where those

technologies converge is where you find truly transformational change. This change is both disruptive and positive, so mentoring people to become those change agents who have the vision to see convergence points and the resulting possibilities and risks for their organization is not only essential but will also lead to true greatness. We need to nurture and grow people who are comfortable with being uncomfortable when making decisions and accepting risk. Growing fearless and successful agents of change is particularly relevant today; creating leaders who excel in harnessing the rapid pace of change and empowering them to take calculated risks to achieve the art of the possible will lead to extraordinary success.

There is no one formula for successful leadership, but there are behaviors and approaches that are repeatable for success across various situations and in any leadership context. The most consistent and pronounced hallmarks of great leaders are seeing their vision through to successful execution, tenacity, integrity, trustworthiness, and thoughtful and persistent mentorship of others. Humility and confidence enable leaders to excel in promoting success in others and in mentoring them to become bold change leaders.

Good leadership is not complicated, but it is deliberate. It can be summed up in three basic principles:

- Inspire and connect
- Find your three positives
- Don't be a jerk

INSPIRE AND CONNECT

Even in this age that is being complicated by accelerating technology, which is making our lives increasingly virtual, leadership is not about machines, formulas, and numbers. It is about people. It is about carbon life-form to carbon life-form interactions.

When I read leadership and management books and they include what appear to be complex mathematical formulas to reinforce some leadership theory, it makes my head implode. We've all been victim to those books, and that misguided effort to add gravitas to some leadership concept through equations really makes me just want to grind a fork in my eyeball. Being composed of about 60 percent water and the rest mathematical antimatter, I just can't relate. For me, leadership is inherently about people and behavior, not formulas and complex theory.

Leadership and mentoring are about developing, inspiring, and leading change with people. Management is about metrics. Thankfully, no calculators will be harmed by reading this book; we will generally avoid the insanity of leadership mathematics.

So I don't disappoint those of you who love a good formula (many of my nerdy friends in this field are squarely—no pun intended—in this camp) and feel that a book in the genre is incomplete without an equation of some sort, I will give you just one so we can get it out of the way.

$$f(x) = a_0 + \sum_{n=1}^{\infty} \left(a_n \cos\cos \tfrac{n\pi x}{L} + b_n \sin\sin \tfrac{n\pi x}{L} \right) = i\,8\,\pi = \text{wtf}^{10}$$

Where i = me

What a beautiful formula. I can see my Frontier Central High math teacher, Mr. Wiley, tearing up now. After two tries at passing trigonometry and barely scraping by with a low C, I celebrated the mission accomplished and the headline "Local girl does good."

All kidding aside, even the most complex leadership challenges can be broken down into common, simple pieces that are solved through human interaction. It involves focusing on and understanding the perspective of others and how to motivate people toward a common outcome. For everything else, you can always eat π.

FIND YOUR THREE POSITIVES

1. Train your brain to be positive and put that into action.
2. Choose to see opportunity and remove barriers; don't be deterred by obstacles. Acknowledge negatives and challenges, then move on, with all effort and focus on the positive outcome.
3. Collaborate and promote positive teamwork.

Just as the best leaders never let a good crisis go to waste, the best leaders are also positive and in constant receival mode, open to diversity of thought and new ideas different from their own. They do not allow ego to get in the way of the humility and humanity necessary to learn from someone else, a mistake, a gaffe, a failure, or another leadership challenge. They don't see blunder, failure, or shortfalls; they see opportunity and will pull positive learning from every experience.

Finding your three positives in any situation is simply a matter of perspective and attitude and the ability to not take yourself too seriously. My life is basically a series of cringe-worthy experiences and gaffes strung together in a continuum of well-crafted and perfected jackassery. But with each of those incidents, I learned something that helped me make better decisions or guide others with a range of options so they could avoid the same misstep.

Sea Stories are anecdotes told by sailors, chiefs, and officers, often embellished over time and with alcohol, that have humor, heart, and some redeeming quality or lesson to be learned. Having spent the last thirty years in the US Navy, I've collected many experiences that illustrate various leadership examples or scenarios. I've often found the best way to talk about them is through stories. Over the years, I've learned that the best way to mentor and lead change is through personal experiences that are relatable and shared rather than just dry leadership theory. Every event in our lives presents a learning opportunity and a nugget to be used in mentoring others. You can use Sea Stories to provide a colorful example of what to do or what not to do as you mentor and lead change. Sometimes even small stories carry big lessons.

Make it a point to pull three positives out of every situation and capture them in your own Sea Stories. The events don't need to be monumental to result in a teaching moment. Be a storyteller. Including Sea Stories in the overall fabric of your leadership—and sharing them with those you mentor—strengthens your shared bonds and makes the lessons easier to remember.

DON'T BE A JERK

We have a general tendency to overcomplicate leadership, but it's actually so easy a monkey could do it. At its core is our third basic tenet: Don't be a jerk. Although we all have potential jerks hiding inside us, great leaders constantly reexamine their behavior and root out the jerk within. They are open to constructive feedback on their leadership style from others, and they act on that feedback to improve.

Think about the best leaders and mentors you've known or had. What was it about them that made you want to follow them, made you want to be like them, or made you loyal to them—not just to their vision but to them as a person? People might get pushed by jerks, but they don't follow them. Good leaders are people you want to follow. That is a testament of respect and of their impact on the lives of others. I don't always get it right, and neither will you. Instead of striving for constant perfection, I acknowledge my flaws and work hard at correcting them. I can be impatient and have a tendency to interrupt or to not be a good listener. You know that annoying person who thinks they know what you are going to say next and is already planning their response? Sadly, that's me. It's something I have to constantly work on and fight against with better active listening techniques.

Growing as a leader requires you to identify your own faults and to take specific actions, not just brush over the flaw. For example, in the case of better listening, one of the best lessons that I've learned with the help of others along the way is to keep eye contact with the person speaking. I try to focus not just on what they are saying but on how they are saying it. This keeps my mind occupied looking for meaning and purpose rather than a response.

You want people to be comfortable coming to you even with the worst news. If you go *Game of Thrones* on them and start lopping off heads, you will hear bad news only once. That is not the type of environment you want to encourage, because you can't fix a problem if you don't know it exists. You need to hear the bad news as well as the good, and you need to hear it sooner rather than later.

Bad news is like stinky cheese: It doesn't get better with time. If you act like a jerk, your people will shut down—and, eventually, so will your business.

Leadership is a bit like chess; it requires strategic thinking and meaningful action. Well-mentored and successful change leaders know how to identify and understand unintended consequences and second- and third-order effects, and how to incorporate those into their efforts and articulate them in their strategic vision. Achieving this type of agile-acting leadership in an organization requires people who are artfully mentored and visibly supported, able to navigate through uncharted waters, transparent and tenacious in pursuit of their vision, and inspirational in collaborating and growing others around them to share those same traits and values. In other words, it requires you to not be a jerk so you can mentor others to also not be jerks.

SIDES OF A COIN

Leadership and mentorship are two sides of the same coin, and you have to be deliberate in your actions to do them well. They both require integrity, empathy, and the ability to inspire others. They require you to excite your team, your employees, and your mentees. You must genuinely connect with other people, clearly and frankly communicating what to expect, how you measure success, and that what you *do* means more than what you *say*. Above all, they both require you to not be a jerk. To that end, I've interwoven leadership and mentoring concepts throughout the book, alternating between chapters but with the intention of showing their interconnectedness and how the best leaders align their efforts in both areas effectively.

ONE

LEAD CHANGE

W e live in an age in which exponentially accelerating and converging technology is fundamentally altering the way we live. The current rate of change can seem daunting and challenging, but it presents opportunities and risks that leaders should seek out and take advantage of. Whereas some people experience a tsunami of uncertainty that can bring discomfort and stress, others thrive on the newness and sense of possibility. Your workforce will be a combination of the two extremes and the middle ground, but they all will look to your leadership for guidance and direction.

Change is exciting but also makes people uncomfortable, as it disrupts the status quo and often flies in the face of conventional wisdom, existing processes, and norms that people have grown used to or built careers around. They can resist change and be blind to the opportunities that come with it. The inability to see the effect a technology can have on business and operational processes has been the demise of many formerly successful companies.

For example, Blockbuster was once the world leader in home video rental. Every home had a VCR, and so instead of packing up the family for a night out at a movie theater, we might rent a half-dozen tapes for the weekend. The home television became the new cinema. When the internet came along, Blockbuster's vision remained in the rearview mirror, and the company missed the boat. Netflix pushed Blockbuster out of the video rental market by allowing customers to find movies from home and have DVDs shipped directly to them. But then Netflix went further, embracing online streaming video and fundamentally transforming how we consume entertainment.

Sears, once the largest retailer in the United States, similarly brought about a sea change and then drowned under the next wave. When Sears began, the home goods industry was stationary. You had to visit a physical store, and your choices were limited to whatever it had in stock. These stores also most likely sold only a single category of items, so, for instance, if you needed both some new bedding and a cooking pot, you'd have to go to two different stores. Then Sears took a risk; it spent a huge sum on print and mailing services instead of on local advertising budgets and sales events. Sears put a catalog in every mailbox, full of every kind of merchandise you could imagine—housewares, appliances, toys, clothing—and the company sailed ahead of its competition and changed the way people shopped. Just a few decades later, catalogs disappeared as online shopping took their place. Sears was left with hundreds of physical stores that no one was visiting, and Amazon ate their lunch. Not only did we no longer have to step into a store, but we also didn't have to wait for a new catalog each month. We could browse for anything we could want from the comfort of our couches and have it delivered directly to our door. The inability of Sears to question its culture and the future relevance of its existing business and to see the opportunity of the convergence of technologies like the internet, big data, and logistics transformation led to its downfall. Timing is everything. When Sears did realize what it needed to do, it was too late to take on the successful behemoths like Amazon.

OPPORTUNITY AND RISK

As you can see, change poses both opportunity and risks to an organization, and how you and your team respond will determine your future. Embracing opportunity—identifying the art of the possible—and being able to combine people, processes, and technology will substantially improve an organization's outcomes. Of course, you may adopt the wrong technology or apply it too quickly without addressing the implications of implementation. Paving the cowpath is also a real danger—that is, using the new technology without the benefit of changing processes and fully embracing the change. The biggest risk may lie in not adopting a technology that could be transformational for your organization and that others will use to gain a competitive advantage. Identifying those converging technologies that are truly transformational is the real game changer, and you need your team trained to think that way.

Ask yourself, *Do I want to be Amazon or Sears? Are we going to be Blockbuster or Netflix?* Being agile means understanding the risk of adopting or not adopting a potentially transformational technology and being able to pivot with the change if need be. You need to plan for the elements of change that accompany a technology's insertion that could lead to success. You need to be comfortable with being uncomfortable. Being a change agent means bringing others along with you. You are the Pied Piper, with a vision for what the future looks like that people can understand, rally behind, and see themselves being a part of.

Vision

Think about recent advances and how they have significantly affected our daily lives. If you had a flip phone fifteen years ago, you were the cool kid, and you might have even received a text message or two. Today, we use our smartphones as sources of limitless information and constant connection and distraction in our pocket. A technology that was, at one point, full of possibilities and challenges now permeates everything.

To successfully keep a business afloat—let alone mentoring others for the future—you need to be attuned to incoming trends and innovation. You must be able to see not just how technology can provide a competitive advantage for your organization now, but how it could change the very nature of leadership, collaboration, information sharing, and how we communicate. True innovations change everything, and only those ready to embrace change can get ahead of the wave.

Vision distinguishes good leaders from great leaders and wildly successful organizations from mediocre ones. When considering technology changes, visionary leaders understand that processes and people must be combined with the technology to make it work. Understanding the possible implications of exponentially accelerating and converging technology can give you a considerable competitive advantage, but you need to integrate this technology and its accompanying process change into your business. You need to be proactive in thinking about how to use it, identifying how it might provide an advantage, and implementing it at speed.

Promote the wild imagination

Ten years ago, no one had heard of Uber, unless you were German and everything was "Uber fantastisch"! Today, not only have most people heard of ride-share services like Uber and Lyft, but those companies have become a part of our daily lives, particularly if you reside in a densely populated area. Forget that old advice from Mom about not getting in the car with strangers. Throw caution to the wind, friends. Ride-shares were able to upset the transportation industry because they are cheaper, faster, and more convenient than the alternatives. Instead of calling a taxi the night before or waiting around for a bus, we can simply tap the Uber app on our smartphone and have a ride to the airport in minutes.

Now, imagine that you combined Uber with an electric, autonomous, self-driving vehicle. That convergence of three powerful technologies would take change and its challenges and opportunities to a whole new level. We would no longer need to wait for a taxi or a bus, we wouldn't have to stop for fuel as frequently (especially if it were solar), and we wouldn't even need a driver. It would revolutionize the transportation industry and how we live.

Imagine a future world where those three technologies converge. This new mode of sustainable, convenient, and automated transportation means that kids born today would never need to learn how to drive a car. They would never own a car. It would mean that, unless the existing business models adapt, there would be no car dealerships, no rental companies, no car parts stores, and no car insurance industry. When I left for work in the morning, I would walk out of my house and a vehicle would be there waiting for me. It could be an autonomous vehicle that looks and acts like the cars we use today, or it could be some kind of hovercraft or pod. (That's the point of letting your imagination go: You don't have to be attached to what came before.) Based on the heuristics of my previous travel behavior, the vehicle would know what time I left every day and where I would be going. I would get in, the vehicle would scan the radio frequency ID in my arm or some other biometric authentication, it would charge my bank a small sum, and it would take me to work. If I needed to go to the airport instead, I would just tell it that and off we would go. Meanwhile, the vehicle would use artificial intelligence agents to scour the internet for information that would be helpful regarding my new destination, and it would provide that to me in the context that it knows would be most useful, presenting it both on a screen in the vehicle and to my smartphone or, eventually, directly to my brain.

Elements of this vision are already happening and much faster than we ever anticipated, so learn to look for the possibilities in a future like this and identify the risks of not adapting at speed (Sears). We already have unprecedented success in ride-sharing services. Self-driving cars and autonomous vehicles have made unprecedented advancements and are statistically safer than human drivers, and who knows what new use for them we'll think of when they're more widely available. The leaders in any industry will be those who can imagine what *could* be, then find a way to quickly make that possibility a reality. If you're the one to successfully bring it to market, look out world!

The only obstacle to innovation and transformation is your imagination, so challenge yourself to see technology as an enabler of transformative ideas. This requires creative thinkers with the imagination to throw off the shackles of old ways of doing business to see a new future. Not everyone has that kind of vision, and if you don't, you should surround yourself with people who do, and create a culture that rewards it. Don't let them be self-limiting in their thinking or get discouraged by institutional inertia or resistance to change. Swiftly help them to remove cultural or institutional barriers for success and publicly reward those who get it right. Take off the blinders and run.

Be an innovator, inspire people to challenge the status quo, and communicate that vision with your teams of employees, stakeholders, and others you collaborate or operate with. This is what distinguishes great leaders from good managers. While there are many factors behind innovation, technology can be a major transformational driver when combined with the accompanying changes affecting people and processes. Lead technology-enabled change by looking for what *could be* with respect to your organization. Discover ways to not only address an existing challenge but also visualize the possibilities. Solve a problem that people don't even realize they have yet.

IMAGINATION TO REALITY

To not only embrace change but lead it, you'll need to inspire people and create processes to encourage innovation. First, you must move quickly. Technology—and any innovation—moves fast; if you drag your feet, you'll be left behind. Next, you'll need crystal-clear communication to get everyone on board—and keep them there. Finally, just as you embraced new ideas and new technology, you must encourage continued innovation in your team. Connect, collaborate, and act—then rinse and repeat.

Make it reality—quickly

You need to demonstrate capability quickly. No one wants to see you admire the problem and show your vision on PowerPoint slides indefinitely. They want to see it in action. They want to touch it, feel it, experience it.

Implement a strategic communication plan

You need to spread the word and get others to do the same using the same concepts and lexicon. This creates consistent messaging and makes the message for the vision clear to everyone involved, regardless of whether they are striving toward the same goal as everyone else. The plan applies to both internal and external communications. Keep your messaging consistent and simple, and tailored to your audience. Use marketing to discuss your change in operational terms that resonate with the audience, not technology geek-speak. Discuss the capability that will result and how operations could be improved with the application of these new technologies. Finally, call out those who get it right publicly. Let everyone know who is being creative and bold in adapting. The key is to make sure everyone understands what you are doing and why it matters.

Pet the cat

As with any comprehensive effort, there will be naysayers, those who remain staunchly opposed—you know, the type of people who spend more time and effort trying to say no when, if they just did it, they would be done already. They are the ones who often cast stones without providing a better solution.

Most often, they are fearful of the change because it upsets their apple cart or may be difficult to convey to their stakeholders and workforce. As a leader in this type of situation, you need to acknowledge that fear and help your team overcome it. I call this part "petting the cat." Imagine a skittish cat on your lap. To keep it there, you need to pet it calmly and encourage it with a soothing "It's going to be OK. Just stick with me here. Don't jump off." Help your people and key stakeholders see their path to alignment with the larger effort for success beyond just their organization.

Even then, you may still face opposition by those with their PhD in institutional resistance who will slow-roll you or be outright obstructionists. If a team member or key stakeholder can't see how to reform their processes fast enough, has a myopic vision of the future or none at all, or is concerned about how the changes will affect them personally, they will be difficult to convince. The way forward is then to understand and acknowledge their angst, especially when they feel it may threaten their vision, resources, money, or people. Give them two shots to come aboard, spending time discussing how the changes could help their programs or capabilities and encouraging them to look beyond their organization to see the greater good. If they still resist, waste no more time with them and tell your team to do the same.

Instead, focus your time and energy on the 20 percent who get it immediately and the 60 percent who sit on the fence but can be pulled to your side. Focus on the positive forces and gather momentum and energy from them. Accept that you will lose that 20 percent who are resisting. Those anchors to progress will eventually be overcome by events when solutions become institutionalized across the enterprise. So, don't waste time on them. They will be dragged along whether they support it or not, and your time is better spent moving forward.

Multitask

An organization-wide change requires leadership throughout the team to have many plates spinning at once. Focus on working toward parallel improvements whenever possible to take advantage of the increased speed this offers—capability on more than one axis. This requires you to reinforce collaboration, cooperation, and strong communication between teams leading different efforts or aspects of the implementation.

Encourage diversity of thought

You can't think of something new if you're doing the same things as everyone else. Be open to new approaches and expect your people to think and act differently. If you mentor them on how to do that, they will. Don't get stuck on old processes or the way things are done. Think about—and have your people think about—what can be jettisoned. Start with new processes from a different angle. This is a completely different way to look at the problem and offers more opportunity for truly transformational thinking and results.

Being truly transformational with technology requires agility to pivot to the next technology, speed to use it quickly, and focused attention to balance multiple efforts simultaneously. Only by embracing change, seeking out new ideas, and leading your team to always move forward can you create the future.

SEA STORY

18 MONTHS TO 24 HOURS

In my last job in the Navy, I started a project called "Compile to Combat in 24 Hours." It was a focused effort to take what I had learned over thirty years and chart the way forward for digital transformation in the Navy. It covered a wide

continued

array of significant changes, including technology insertion (such as new ways to develop and field applications, the use of commercial cloud technologies, data standardization for improved usage and cybersecurity protection, and laser and light fidelity for communications), policy and process changes, and improvements in how we used our workforce. It was an all-encompassing enterprise-level effort to go after key fundamental changes to the Navy's architecture, infrastructure, people skills, policy, and processes. The task was monumental but necessary. Stabs had been taken in the past to go after parts of it, but it needed a holistic enterprise perspective and vision, a solution with actionable plans, and execution in phases. Even with the most complex plans, you eat the elephant a little at a time and you eventually get there.

Quick implementation

To get things moving, our team picked the modernization of secure application development in the cloud (including the process reform of getting capability fielded more quickly by removing administrative and bureaucratic barriers to speed) and testing of light fidelity for networking aboard ship. With the help of a fantastically bright team of innovators led by the brilliant Delores Washburn, the chief engineer and director of Tactical Systems Engineering and Integration at Naval Information Warfare Center Pacific, Rear Admirals Kurt Rothenhaus and Carl Chebi, and many others, we validated both of those capabilities during a pilot demonstration on two Navy ships within eight months of starting the project.

We achieved this by discovering and leveraging smaller efforts already in the works that were folded in, as they fit with the technology and process changes we were making. The extraordinary creativity, energy, drive, and dedication of the team helped improve the Navy's information environment. We focused the pilot tests on key portions of technology and process implementation that we could demonstrate quickly, continue to learn lessons from and build on, and use to gain more momentum.

Strategic communications

People had attempted to fix different pieces of the Navy architecture and processes over the years, but that eating-around-the-edge approach was not solving the problem holistically. A holistic approach was required to build what we needed for the future, so that is where I focused my time and energy. We understood that in fixing the hard problems, people could stop focusing on the issues caused by not having a solution in place and they could do more meaningful work. This approach needed consistent, persistent leadership reiterating the vision for the future, visibly knocking down barriers that slowed forward momentum, and challenging everyone to see their part and be equally aggressive in shifting the heading of the ship in the right direction. I told the team repeatedly that we were going to be relentless in our efforts, regardless of how slow the organization tended to move. We were going to ride the enterprise like Seabiscuit to get them to move at a faster pace than they

continued

were comfortable with. Being uncomfortable was the new comfortable—a new normal for everyone.

Now, a big organization like the Navy has many *silos of excellence,* in which good work may be done in a limited fashion, but they don't always align to a larger vision, particularly when the larger vision has changed and the existing programs continue to plod along on a traditional path. Technology, in this case, was a disrupter that fundamentally forced change and a rethinking of what could be if we could get beyond our existing programs and ways of doing business. Many of the existing plans had been developed in a different time under a different set of circumstances and were no longer relevant. Exponentially accelerating and converging technology had made possible options that were only dreamed of a few short years ago, and the Navy needed to get aboard to retain a competitive advantage over our adversaries.

That is easy to say but hard to do in a big bureaucracy that, most days, moves like a glacier on Ritalin. Even explaining the vision in plain English and not in information technology dolphin-speak was a challenge. Like a pig staring at a wristwatch, people didn't immediately see how they fit into the vision or what they needed to do or change. We had to break it down and put the effort into language with specifics that they understood. We had to create a clear context in which they could see that they had an important role to play.

It was an exhausting slog every day fighting the forces of institutional resistance, but I had expected that, so I girded my loins and just went after it, plowing through or going around obstacles and resistance. I decided to make the project my number one priority because I knew that it was what the Navy needed most, no matter how hard it was going to be to get there. I never veered from that priority and reinforced it in every conversation with my team and with my boss. I found hope and encouragement from people across the enterprise who got it early on and were all in to help. Those were the forces of change that I latched on to like grim death, and I discovered there were champions in many areas to move the effort forward.

All aboard

I am not one to take counsel from naysayers. I will listen to a counterview, and if they have a better idea, I am happy to jump aboard their train. However, those who just wish to derail an idea while presenting no other alternatives should be left behind at the station. I knew that this project was going to need support from key stakeholders both inside and outside the Navy, and we needed to demonstrate capability for several elements of the solution so that people could have a tangible to latch on to. I had a good feel for the organization's tolerance for risk (not very high) and identified those points where we were going to really push the envelope, and we did.

One example of this was in transforming old processes that would no longer apply in this new environment. The entire team and I worked very hard to have those organizations take their old processes and throw them out the window. They were challenged to envision a new process in

continued

this changed environment that achieved their objectives but in a much more rapid and cybersecure manner. Many of these process owners were from different commands across the Navy and had different responsibilities and interests. This required sustained and engaged leadership on both sides to ensure each side understood the end-state vision and what each group's role was in getting the Navy there. Frank communication about the challenges and concerns along the way was paramount at multiple levels in each organization. Removing roadblocks and barriers to success was a team effort. One of those processes was for obtaining approvals to load software on ships. We engaged those process owners early in our development and had them work with us to make parallel changes that would help them deliver capability quickly while saving time and money. We also used them to help with internal resistance to the change where people felt threatened or that the old process still needed to be used to ensure things were "done right." In the end, those process owners significantly reduced the time it took to approve loading software on ships in a new automated model that allows for capability to be delivered to operational forces faster and cheaper.

Spinning plates

The team had to work multiple different elements in parallel, simultaneously spinning many plates like a circus act, to ensure that nothing fell and broke and that they all converged for success. Many factors had to be considered, changed, and refocused in terms of policy, governance, and funding for the effort to work. The following four key pillars were identified and communicated repeatedly and consistently to ensure the vision was understood and that everyone focused on implementation:

1. Development of a data strategy and how data would be moved between Navy ships and the shore information technology infrastructure

2. How all processes for developing and operating computer code could be accomplished rapidly and in a way that incorporated the best cybersecurity practices from the beginning

3. How processes would be automated so they could be done quickly without human intervention and approvals slowing up delivery of the computer code to Navy ships

4. How to use commercial cloud technologies to speed up computer code development and leveraging advanced tools to improve data use

Each pillar represented a large undertaking incorporating hundreds of people and action items by key stakeholders and partners to succeed. Some of these tasks had serial dependencies—one task would need to be accomplished before something else could start. Many could be done in parallel but with close coordination due to overlapping areas of responsibility or governance.

The entire team worked diligently to keep these many plates spinning at once. They ensured alignment of those forces to successfully execute the pilot and provide a roadmap

continued

for implementing the changes on a broader enterprise scale in the future. The entire effort required leadership to reinforce collaboration, cooperation, strong communication, and a focus on the greater good of achieving success for the Navy enterprise. Persistent, tenacious leadership was necessary to ensure strong collaboration between teams leading different aspects of each pillar. Not everything worked as planned, but where we were unable to realize a successful change or capability, we kept at it even after the pilot was successfully demonstrated to ensure long-term implementation.

Think differently

I had to personally get our team to think differently, and they stepped up to the task with great results. For the first pilot, which focused on application delivery to a ship, I knew we would have to transform existing processes, or the whole thing would not work. One process addressed a series of tests and documentation that were part of a software approval process. The process was important to make sure we addressed cybersecurity and functional concerns; we couldn't risk breaking the ship with new software. The existing approval process was bloated and took about eighteen months, required a lot of human intervention, and frankly, didn't apply to the new agile software development and delivery model we had devised.

I challenged the team in our first month together to change that process and come back to me with how they would take it from eighteen months to twenty-four hours with no human in the loop. I told them we had to be able to do it fast and with the right cybersecurity controls in place but left the solution wide open for them to be creative.

When I said twenty-four hours, I could see heads imploding throughout the room, but they got after it, and a few weeks later, they enthusiastically reported that they had reduced the time of the process from eighteen months to twelve months.

I told them, "Wrong denominator: twenty-four hours. Go back and work it again."

Right away, I could see they were disappointed, so we stopped at that point and discussed a different approach. They had been taking their old process for approving software application delivery and trying to morph it using the new processes we had developed for agile software application development and delivery. I told them to start with a blank sheet of paper and identify those minimum controls needed using the new development and delivery processes— and then build the new approval process around those.

Two weeks later, the team reconvened. They had come up with a process that worked in the twenty-four-hour window and met the minimum controls. We tested the first iteration in the pilot, and it worked. More work needed to be done to make it even better, but the point is that the technology enabled process reform, and out-of-the-box thinking by a creative team was the combination that proved truly transformational.

Change within change

We expected we would have things that didn't work perfectly or that were only a 60 percent solution for the pilot.

continued

We did not punish failure; we learned from our missteps and made improvements. The specific initiatives ultimately morphed into other efforts that continued their momentum and became even stronger. In the process, we grew teams of innovators across the Navy and reinforced good behaviors and learned how to be more collaborative, agile, and nimble. As technology advancement cycles become more compressed and the capabilities more astounding, having people who start with the "clean sheet of paper" mentality is the foundation for significant organizational transformation.

THREE POSITIVES

1. We learned from both success and failure and used them both as jumping-off points for future success.

2. We set bold, audacious goals and did our best to meet them.

3. We never let professional resistance wear us down.

TWO

WHY
MENTORING
MATTERS

When you see a turtle on a fence post, you know it didn't get there on its own. No one is a success by themselves. There is always someone behind the scenes advocating on your behalf, even if you aren't aware of it.

I have always felt like a little kid learning to ride a bike—all excited and proud—when I accomplish something. But every achievement was made with the great support of family, friends, and mentors who plowed obstacles out of my way. They also held the back of the bike until I was steady enough to balance. I just had to keep pedaling.

A good mentor supports you and guides you on your path. They know when to listen and when to give advice. They are a good sounding board for ideas or can help you work through a tough leadership or ethical situation. They look for opportunities for you and support your advancement and professional progress with others. They don't give you the answers; they teach you to think through the problem to find the answer yourself. They talk to you about options you should consider in the calculus of the decision you will make and the possible consequences of choosing one of those options over another. In short, they lift you up and make your success as much of a priority as—or more than—their own. Having a good mentor can change your life personally and professionally.

But the cyclist isn't the only one who learns something from that bike ride; the one pushing them does too. Being a mentor for others is incredibly rewarding, but it takes a lot of work, attention, and thought. You have to grow your relationship over time, building trust between you and your mentee. If you are any good, you'll be with your mentee through thick and thin, and you'll tell them what they need to hear, not what they want to hear. You will challenge your mentee and be challenged in return so that you grow together. Just like your success was supported and enabled by your trusted friends, your mentee's success reflects their own hard work—and yours.

WHAT MAKES A GOOD MENTOR?

I often ask groups, "What makes someone a good mentor?" The responses circle around several key factors. I have learned over the years that while there are many traits that make great mentors, these factors consistently surface as priorities for people who have a successful mentor-mentee relationship.

A good mentor is someone who is successful in what you want to achieve and who provides professional advice and frank feedback. A good mentor understands you and your personal and professional goals and challenges you to think beyond what you see yourself achieving. A good mentor is a good listener; sometimes, all a person needs is someone else to listen. A good mentor teaches you to judge your success by your own goals and effort, not by comparing yourself to someone else. A good mentor helps you to see opportunity when a door is closed or when the work landscape has shifted unexpectedly.

A good mentor is accessible and will discuss whatever topic or decision their mentee needs, with open and transparent communication. They offer advice that you need to hear, not necessarily what you want to hear—and that may not always be easy—for either of you. A good mentor helps you to think through your actions and decisions but doesn't give you the answer. They teach you how to get there yourself and to recognize what the broader implications and the potential second- and third-order effects of your decision could be.

A good mentor lifts others up. They do not try to make you into them. Rather, they help you achieve your personal best and your goals. They want to make you more successful than they are, and they seek out and recommend opportunities for you. They understand and convey the finer points of great leadership, like humility, tenacity, grace, courage, teamwork, collaboration, and empathy. They see you for who you are and help you become the best version of yourself you can be.

If you've had any significant success in your career, you likely had an excellent mentor or two. What did they do to help you along the way? Put that into practice and mentor someone else.

THE MENTOR MESH

It would be unusual to have just one mentor, and I wouldn't recommend anyone rely on one individual to guide them through their life and career. You should have what I call a *mentor mesh*, a fabric of multiple mentors guiding your development over the years. As you move through your career, you may change jobs and even professions and will have significant events in your personal life that are helped by having mentors who understand those situations in the context of your life and goals and can provide insight.

It is realistic and plausible that a mentee can actually outgrow their mentor as well, as their career advances and they move to positions that eclipse where their mentor has been. That's OK. The mentor may have been a good source of professional advice up to a certain point, but once they no longer have the insight to provide advice at the higher level to guide you, they can transition into another role, like friend. You can still remain close with them to provide you advice in other aspects of your career and life in which their experience is still relevant. For example, they may not be able to give advice on strategic enterprise planning or risk management, but they can still give wise counsel on other leadership challenges like having difficult conversations, addressing organizational change, resolving an ethical dilemma, taking yourself less seriously, or dealing with work-life balance.

In my career, I've formed my own mentor mesh. For example, I have some senior mentors who help me tremendously by providing advice on issues of a corporate or strategic nature. I also have technical mentors, subject matter experts in my fields, who provide outstanding advice on technical matters or ideas I am thinking about pushing forward in the organization. I also have mentors who have successfully juggled nontraditional careers with being a mom in the military. They navigated those tough waters of family separations, deployments, and how to stay connected and engaged with their children even when away serving in operational assignments—something that was very important to me to get right. Additionally, there are people who have served as my mentors for more than twenty years who, while they did not advance as far in the organization from a leadership perspective as I did, they are superior leaders with advice that is invaluable for dealing with a tough situation. I am grateful to have the benefit of continued counsel and wisdom from all of them.

Listening to advice from experienced mentors helps you to navigate potentially shallow waters. They may be in your organization and can observe you firsthand and discreetly provide advice, or they may be outside your organization and you meet with them to describe what is going on and ask for advice. Each of my mentors provides unique and valuable advice that enriches my life and makes me think more critically. Stitched together, their advice provides a patchwork quilt of life and career advice that I treasure. Each patch has significance and adds to the completeness of the quilt. A missing patch is a promise or opportunity unfulfilled. Leaders take those pieces and pay them forward, passing those lessons and advice on to those we mentor as they create their own quilt.

As you select the best traits from your mentor mesh to establish your own mentoring style, remember it is not one-size-fits-all. You will have to tailor your advice and style a bit based on the personality, needs, and goals of the person you are mentoring. Be careful of trying to apply the exact same approach or advice to everyone. Some lessons will be repeatable; other advice will not.

As we discussed, mentors come in all shapes and sizes and with different experiences, and you will likely have multiple mentors for different aspects of your career and life. Those will shift and grow over time as well. So there are many factors to consider when mentoring others and when selecting a mentor for yourself, and not all mentoring relationships will work out. As the relationship matures, if the chemistry is not there, it should be the unwritten rule on both sides that no harm, no foul, you just move on. All good mentors know and practice that rule.

MENTOR IN YOUR FIELD

One mentoring trait that mentees look for is someone who has been successful in their chosen field. They want to learn from someone who has the street cred of experience and perspective on what is important to succeed in that line of work. While your mentor mesh will likely include several mentors, at least one of them should be in your area of specialization. Some mentors can provide advice that crosses industry, agnostic of career field (like leadership and work-life balance), but a mentor with experience and insight into the mentee's career of choice is crucial.

There is a long-standing joke at the National Security Agency (NSA), an organization filled with some of the most dedicated and brilliant scientific minds in the nation, that an introvert at NSA looks at their shoes and an extrovert looks at yours. In information technology, we joke about the tinfoil hat, dolphin-speak crowd, but computer programming and technology-heavy fields do attract a certain type of person who thrives in that environment. So be attuned to the culture of your industry as a mentor and learn how you can make your mentee aware of that culture as a factor in how they make decisions and move forward and how they lead and mentor others in that industry.

People tend to gravitate toward career fields and cultures that fit their personality in general, but that is not always the case, and where there is a mismatch, the mentee can get frustrated. When there is a disconnect, you can help them work through specific actions they can take to make the situation more manageable, or in the end, they may decide that they are not a good fit for the industry. Those discussions should center on what aspects of the culture the mentee struggles with and how those affect their performance or future potential. Advise them on ways they can manage their own behavior so they don't become frustrated or demoralized. Identify specific indicators of culture that can be positively changed and those that cannot. Can your mentee still thrive if there are aspects they cannot change?

I have found the best approach is to have mentees write down a prioritized list of behaviors that may be industry- or institution-specific that they struggle with, then have them assess which they think they can change or manage. Then we go through what management actions they will take and how they will determine if those actions, once taken, are having the desired effect.

Your mentee should take care to not attribute a one-off problem (e.g., a bad boss) as an organizational or career-field cultural problem, so discussing their list regarding the source of the problem is important. Some cultural problems require much more effort to course-correct—for example, the #MeToo movement to combat sexual harassment—but the mentee can still be a powerful part of the solution. That teaches them to grow as a leader and to think beyond their immediate personal struggle to how they can effect change for the greater good.

This is not to imply that there are only negatives here. There are often good cultural aspects to communities and professions that you will want to highlight for your mentees. Some industries have very good formal mentoring or professional development programs (e.g., lawyers, real estate agents, welders). These can be formal apprenticeships, professional associations, or internship programs, or they can be informal but part of the evolved culture of the profession (e.g., academics, electricians). Regardless of the format, they are intended to lift others up and enable their success, and good mentors will connect their mentees with these groups. You can use your interpersonal network to recommend your mentee for opportunities to seek out avenues to increase their professional visibility through participating in career-related activities and events, publishing articles, speaking at conferences, and even in getting jobs.

HELP MENTEES NAVIGATE THE GRAY ZONE

In a majority of cases, there is no one right answer, and you should tell your mentees that. In leadership, we live in the gray zone between obviously black or white. I have very rarely come across a situation with only one right answer. Teach your people how to navigate through the gray to come up with the best possible answer. This will help them see the world more realistically. The higher you advance in an organization, the more you will live in the gray and will be relied on for your experience, judgment, and intellect to navigate with purpose and thoughtfulness through it. That means being comfortable with being uncomfortable, making decisions with the best facts and advice available, taking calculated risks with known information gaps and seams, and being decisive. Teach your mentees not to allow the gray zone to exist simply because they or someone else doesn't want to make a tough decision. As leaders, our job is to make those tough decisions. Providing your mentee with the opportunity and advice to think through problems themselves helps them build confidence in their effectiveness for leading through the gray zone.

BEING A GOOD MENTOR

We all borrow from the best and learn from the worst for how we will act when we are put in positions of increased responsibility. Look for opportunities to harvest both kinds of lesson—what to do and what *not* to do—from the leaders you come across. Even the worst leaders, the jerks, can teach you something—how you will never treat someone else. Building and continuing to strengthen your mentorship skills is important so you can lead your team on a larger scale as you move up in an organization. You can use your position for greater influence and actions benefiting others and, on a smaller scale, those you connect with individually.

Being a good mentor takes time and effort, but as a leader, it is the most important thing you will do. For all the professional accomplishments you achieve, which may seem significant at the time, many are forgotten to history. But how you touched someone's life, how you made it better through the time you spent providing guidance and helping them achieve success, will never be forgotten. In many cases, your mentoring will become a part of their leadership toolkit and will be passed on to those they mentor in the same way. By paying it forward, we are each exponentially helping the leaders of the future.

Does anyone remember who was vice president of the United States in 1888? Who won the Olympic curling gold medal in 1984? Who was the top-selling recording artist in 1929? Who won the Nobel Prize for medicine in 1966? Who won the Nathan's Hot Dog Eating Contest in 2011? (That last one was Joey Chestnut, with sixty-two hot dogs, but I had to look it up . . . then I sucked down some Mylanta just thinking about it.) The point is those people were at the top of their game, but for all of their effort and accomplishment in their respective fields of excellence (yes, that includes eating hot dogs), those accomplishments are largely forgotten in time or overcome by other events. The same will be true of most of our accomplishments that, in the moment, seem to carry such weight or importance. What matters in the long run are the people we connect with and how we can enrich their lives. Mentoring is our way of doing just that: looking for ways to make someone successful and feel important. That is what will be remembered when it matters: the people whose lives are changed for the better by that mentorship.

SEA STORY

DO WHAT IS RIGHT, EVEN WHEN NO ONE IS LOOKING

I have two examples to highlight here. In the first case, I worked with a Navy admiral who upheld the highest standards of ethical behavior. She always took time to mentor her subordinates and to ensure that we learned how to think through often tough decisions. She would remind us that just because something was legal did not mean it was

continued

the right thing to do because of the message it might send. Our judgment and strong moral compass must kick in to look at the action in the greater context.

For example, in the military, when we fly on commercial airlines, we fly in economy class whether we are a seaman or an admiral, because we must remain good stewards of taxpayer money. Many admirals travel extensively due to the nature of their jobs and accrue frequent flyer miles that would allow them to bump up their class of service without any additional cost to the government. While it may be legal to use those frequent flyer miles to bump up to business class, there are people who would see an admiral (in uniform or not, you get recognized) and wonder why the government was buying them a business class ticket. The perception would reflect negatively on the service, so this is just not something that we would choose to do.

In the second case, the Navy had suffered through a recent scandal—a failure of leadership by senior officers and department civilians that was a stain on the service. The scandal involved a civilian contractor named Leonard Glenn "Fat Leonard" Francis. Francis routinely pursued senior commissioned and enlisted Navy leaders in the Pacific theater with bribes of cash, hotel rooms, prostitutes, expensive dinners, and other gifts to get inside information on their ships' schedules or to gain a competitive advantage for ship husbanding and port services contracts. His actions resulted in multiple resignations and criminal convictions, including his own.

These officers felt a misplaced sense of entitlement because of their rank or position. Their actions humiliated themselves and the Navy and were not reflective of the highest integrity, ethics, and judgment found throughout the rest of the US Navy. They do demonstrate how those with low self-esteem, hubris, arrogance, and a misplaced sense of entitlement can lead to exceptionally poor judgment that becomes a cancer on the entire organization.

Navy leaders are instructed on the pitfalls of Bathsheba Syndrome in leadership training. The syndrome's name refers to the biblical story of King David using his powerful position as leader of Israel to send one of his soldiers to war knowing he was facing certain death, so that he could be romantically involved with the man's wife, Bathsheba. Once Bathsheba Syndrome takes hold in an individual, it is normally a slow, steady downward progression of abuse of leadership positions and covering their tracks for some advantage. This normally happens where ethical failure comes after years of successful leadership or where behavior was exhibited on a smaller scale and was never stopped by anyone, so the person became emboldened and felt untouchable.

The progress does not normally happen overnight; rather, it is a slow erosion of the strong values, culture, and integrity that the organization espouses. Excuses are made by the individual and those around them: "Oh, that's just the way she is" or "She is not doing anything illegal" or "Everybody is doing it; I've seen worse." It is facilitated along the way by leaders who remove those who challenge them and

continued

surround themselves with a circle of sycophants and yes-men or -women. When no one is willing to tell the emperor she has no clothes, the organization is officially adrift.

THREE POSITIVES

1. Your integrity and reputation are your own, but your actions are likely influenced by your leaders and mentors—and you can influence the actions of your own mentees.

2. Remember, the more senior you get in an organization, the more important it is to remain humble and to share that value with your teams.

3. Be grateful for everything you have and the ability to use your leadership to influence for the better.

+ + +

You set and maintain your standards throughout your lifetime, and the way you act influences those around you. Never compromise on your high standards and those you expect from your followers. The reputation you build through your ethical actions and decision-making will help you weather any storm. Behave like you are entitled to nothing, and hold yourself, your peers, and the organization to the highest ethical standards. One way to check a team member's or mentee's rudder is to have mentoring discussions using role-based scenarios where you get them to think through ethical dilemmas and describe how they would respond to those in a constructive way. Use this discussion to connect with your ethics and values and to determine those of your mentee.

THREE

MANAGING EXPECTATIONS

E xceptional leaders set clear expectations and help others achieve those goals. They ensure that their teams understand their vision and objectives and what each person needs to contribute as part of the team to meet those high standards. To be a good leader, your expectations must reflect your values. Priorities will change, but your values will not. Establishing a high bar encourages people to reach beyond what they thought possible, and allowing for stumbles along the way shows them you understand that they may struggle in meeting those expectations and where you can jump in to help.

As a leader, you should be as clear as possible about your vision, desires, and expectations. Have you ever had a boss who wants you to do something but doesn't have the vision or understanding to know what they really want or can't articulate it? You know the leaders who say, "Bring me a rock," so you present them with a rock that you think they would like, and they say, "No, not that rock! I want a different rock." So you bring a different rock. Then they say, "No, not that rock either! I want a different rock. I will know it when I see it." They cannot or will not articulate what rock they want.

This type of poor articulation of vision and expectation leads to frustration, confusion, and wasted time and resources as people try to guess what they should be doing. It also leads to low morale; employees feel constantly flat-footed, like they are performing poorly, when in reality, they have not been provided the guidance to succeed. They were set up for failure.

Sometimes, you may want your employees to be creative because you are out of ideas or don't see a clear path forward and would like to get the collective intellect of the organization rallied around coming up with a creative solution. In these cases, you should clearly state that. Be open to trying ideas the team suggests and willing to accept failure if it doesn't work the first time.

In these types of situations, tell the team that you don't know exactly what you want but that you would like to have three or four options that they come up with to choose from. Then pick the best one and go with it, even if it is not one that you would have come up with yourself. Make sure you discuss the options, the team's assumptions, the risks, the resources needed, and the pros and cons of each recommendation and its outcomes to make the best possible choice. Push your team to be bold and come up with options that run the gamut from conservative to audacious, with more risk involved but potentially greater payoff.

You also need to be unambiguous when it comes to roles, responsibilities, and accountability. You can't have everyone in charge or no one in charge. This is particularly painful if it is a result of poor leadership and an inability to make difficult staffing decisions. This can be complicated in matrix organizations, where someone could have multiple bosses. Be cautious of the matrix approach; it is doable but requires very strong leadership; extra attention to collaboration, coordination, and communication; and expectation management by all involved. Also, make sure that what is driving that type of management arrangement is a business or mission need and not a reluctance by leadership to make hard staffing decisions. There needs to be a clear chain of command—whether you use a matrix system or standard management. Codifying that structure for the team, both in an organizational chart that delineates who works for whom and in individual position descriptions, is important to alleviate confusion, ambiguity, frustration, duplication of effort, and other inefficiencies. The lines of authority and where responsibility lies for key functions should be well defined for everyone in the organization.

Creating and sustaining a culture of accountability is important, and that needs to be made clear in your expectations. When expectations and standards have been set and acknowledged, everyone on the team is accountable to them. "I own it" should be part of the corporate value system and demonstrated in every employee's daily activity—especially yours. Even something as simple as walking by a piece of trash outside the front of your building and not picking it up sends a message about the standards you accept. The standard you walk by is the standard you accept. If you allow Joe Bag of Donuts to do something that lowers one of your standards and expectations, you have just made it acceptable throughout the organization. Accept nothing less than the best and hold everyone on the team accountable. The corporate culture you expect should be one where everyone supports the mission and nothing at the organization is someone else's problem.

I have always found that writing down my expectations and providing those to subordinates is beneficial. Everyone should know their role and how they contribute to the mission. For years, I have provided my team with a document that clearly lists the expectations that work for me (an example of which I've included in the appendix). People that I have given this document to have expressed appreciation for not having to guess my values, priorities, and leadership style. Because establishing expectations is a two-way street, I use the expectations document to glean from them and document their expectations of me as well, like an informal contract. They receive the document early in our relationship and we discuss it. It codifies what I expect of my subordinates and what they can expect of me. It gives me a chance to make sure I am clear on their expectations of me and how I can exceed them.

People like to know what is expected of them, in terms of both how they perform individually and how they contribute as a team member. How you meet their expectations is crucial to building and keeping a dedicated workforce. You will reward the behavior you want repeated, so it is best to set out those criteria early and reinforce them with periodic feedback on how well they are meeting your expectations. Define and discuss team members' metrics for success, how their performance will be judged, and how they will be informed if their performance falls short in time to course-correct before it becomes a crisis.

Your expectations document should also include your personal preferences for how you like to be informed about issues, your briefing and communication styles, your ethical standards, and pet peeves to avoid. A pet peeve that I always include is that if I ask a yes-or-no question, I prefer that people provide the yes-or-no answer and then they can get into the *War and Peace* discussion about all of the extenuating circumstances or additional information to make the answer more complete. But give me the yes or no first so I have a clear answer.

The expectations document is not intended to limit creativity, recommendations for new ways to improve processes or outcomes, or the ability to change aspects of the organization that may need it. It is merely a tool to help my employees understand my values and objectives, their respective swim lanes, and how they can be most successful in their roles. While it provides specifics, it is also flexible enough to accommodate changes. I normally revise the document annually or when there are any big organizational changes, such as a significant shift in mission or reprioritization of effort, a large employee turnover, or an external force that impacts the organization positively or negatively (e.g., the shift to remote work due to the coronavirus in 2020).

Refer to the expectations document in the appendix and create your own, with your expectations of your team clearly laid out. You may find my version lengthy, but I have found that all employees I discussed it with appreciated the clarity and level of detail. Whether it's long or short, be *clear.*

EXPECT PEOPLE TO THINK AND ACT STRATEGICALLY

Part of your responsibility as a leader in times of change is to guide and train your team and your mentees to think and act strategically. The higher they advance in an organization, the more they will be expected to know how to think at a strategic level and identify what matters most for mission accomplishment in the context of a larger ecosystem. How will their vision and actions transform, improve, or possibly damage the enterprise? This comes more naturally to some people than it does to others, so gauge where those you lead are in their development as leaders and specifically with respect to their ability to think and act strategically. This means focusing on practical behaviors and reinforcing them in each team member's everyday work. Help them see patterns in complex situations and how those support overarching objectives. Make sure they step outside their comfort zone to learn different functional areas of the organization, not just their own, and how those efforts should align for maximum effectiveness. Have them acknowledge key stakeholders and influencers, and teach them how to find common ground without diluting what needs to be done for mission excellence. Each individual should understand that you don't need 100 percent consensus and sometimes *no* is an acceptable answer.

They must be attuned to their words and actions and to the importance of having those in alignment. Have them discuss their vision and values and how those align with the greater organization so that their teams do not become confused, disconnected, or disillusioned. They should be able to explain their strategic plan, discuss what changes are needed and why, and detail how they will combine the people, processes, technology, and resources to make it happen. Their discussion should also include how they intend to differentiate between their short-term achievable objectives and their long-term goals. They should articulate how they have created a team environment in which everyone understands their role in supporting those objectives and where accountability lies. Reinforce with them that their actions in supporting the implementation of their strategic plan will be more important than their words, so have them convey in action-oriented terms how they are moving forward. They should be able to translate their vision into actionable chunks of effort that can be completed, measured, and seen.

SEA STORY

A HARD LESSON IN ORGANIZATIONAL CHANGE

I was at a large organization that was going through a major change. We were consolidating responsibilities for three other large organizations, realigning functions, and restructuring reporting procedures and duties. All of this was incredibly stressful for the entire team. In addition, the organization had already been reorganized and renamed two previous times in a span of three years. It was a lot of turmoil and reorg fatigue.

The workforce was primarily middle-aged, many prior military, and most had been with the organization in one

continued

form or another for at least ten years. The previous reor-
ganizations had not gone as well as advertised, and the
scar tissue was fresh. There was an atmosphere of skep-
ticism at best and distrust at worst that this time would be
any more successful. Some had been personally affected,
especially those that had not achieved a desired position.
Some had been told some positive effect would come of
the change, and because it didn't, they were not happy that
more change was on the way and were not shy about voic-
ing their concerns. They saw this next reorganization as just
more shuffling deck chairs on the *Titanic.*

This time was different, though, because some jobs were
going to be eliminated. Not the people but the job: We would
find another job for the person, but that might have to be in
another department or even another organization. I knew
that overcommunicating what was happening and addressing their concerns would be paramount to maintaining trust
through what we knew would be a tough time for the organization and all of our teammates working there.

People get emotionally attached to their job and their
work because it makes up such a significant portion of
their life. When a job is eliminated, even for reasons of efficiency or because a merger with another organization makes
that position redundant, the person can feel that their work is
not valued or that they, personally, are not valued.

I was responsible for working through a lot of details of
the reorganization and executing them. I was very conscious
of the resulting angst, and we worked hard to be transparent and openly communicate frequently to the workforce on

what was happening, what was planned, and how it would affect them. These messages had to address the personal as well as the mission challenges. Strategic communication from the boss and anyone in a position of leadership was key, as was ensuring we got frequent feedback.

All that sounds good, right? Well, in execution, it wasn't enough, and I could have done better. We conducted a command climate survey about a month after the reorganization, and I was surprised and saddened when some of the comments came back negatively on the transparency of our efforts: We could have communicated better, and some people expressed concern that they did not understand why things were transpiring as they were. I and the entire senior leadership team thought we had done well, but I had missed the mark.

We knew going in that communication and specificity in addressing workforce concerns would be key. I thought we had communicated the messages clearly and frequently through emails, in-person "town hall" meetings, supervisor-led smaller meetings, and rapid responses to notes dropped in anonymous suggestion boxes. We could have done better on our internal strategic communications by putting out even more frequent written status updates, discussing upcoming events, having more opportunities for group discussions that offered back-and-forth dialogue to clear the air on issues, and providing more detail on how we were going to address unresolved issues between the three organizations being consolidated. The communication could have come three days a week instead of once in a

continued

more ad hoc nature. We also could have been more specific in letting people know the exact nature of the problems we were struggling to find consensus on. That may have led to crowdsourcing a better solution.

I should have also asked for more feedback from the supervisors, not of general complaints, which we were hearing a lot of, but of individual concerns raised that were causing stress or disgruntlement. That would have reinforced that the supervisors were actively engaging with all of their employees at the individual level and would have raised issues that might not have been unique to one person—issues that we needed to address for the entire organization. We also should have done a rudder check or survey of how the entire team perceived how things were going during the reorganization instead of waiting until we were done to find out we could have done better. Bottom line: In a situation like this, you cannot overcommunicate, and not just on organization-level issues, but also in dealing with individual concerns at the supervisor level.

In the command climate survey at the end, two or three comments called me out personally for being a bully. After the initial shock and feeling sad that I had caused someone to feel that way, I took those comments to heart and reflected on what I could have done better or differently. I know that I have certain behaviors that I have to consciously work to not exhibit—interrupting, impatience, swearing. Even for a sailor, I have taken swearing to an art form, and I use the f-bomb like Picasso uses a paintbrush: It's my medium, although I don't swear or yell at people; it's just part of my normal speech. Those traits are not helpful and don't demonstrate good leadership.

While I don't suffer fools, nor should anyone, and I hold people accountable to do their jobs, which some resent, I realize that I can push people too hard. Everyone does not operate at the same speed or intensity, and I need to recognize when I am expecting something that they are not able to deliver at the pace I want. That is not to say you don't work to establish stretch goals or to try to get people to realize they may be capable of more than they think. It can be very rewarding for a person to achieve something that they never felt they could do. But there is a big difference in getting them there in a positive way and pushing someone too far with negative consequences for them and the organization. Be aware of how your words and actions can have a positive effect to inspire attainment of a stretch goal or a negative effect of demoralizing a good worker and making them feel they are underperforming by not meeting your expectations, which may have been unrealistic to begin with. It's a fine line, and as a leader you need to choose your words, then monitor the situation carefully. In this case, I needed to step back and walk a mile in their shoes.

It's not enough to acknowledge your shortcomings. You need to do something about them. After that incident, I worked hard every day on being a better listener (still a big challenge for me), on being more attuned to what people are capable of and putting them in roles where they can succeed, pushing folks to see what they can achieve without pushing them over the edge, and being more patient or letting things

continued

go that won't matter in the long run. If, in three years, no one will remember or care, then don't worry about it.

Successful change involves everyone and requires trust in the leadership to address concerns through demonstrable actions. Frequent, clear communication is key. Understanding personal strengths and weaknesses is an important part in making the entire team successful, and that takes effort, but it is effort well spent. Ultimately, your mission is the most important thing, but you can best achieve your objectives that support that mission by truly understanding and taking care of the members of your team.

THREE POSITIVES

1. Someone made me aware of how I could be a better leader, and I took that criticism to heart and hopefully did improve.

2. I learned important lessons about how to hold people accountable without the kind of pressure that makes them ineffective, that not everyone operates at warp speed, and that finding the best place in an organization is not always as simple as plugging a name into an organizational chart.

3. I gained a clearer understanding of the effect that organizational change has on each individual in a different way.

+ + +

FOUR

FRANK CONVERSATIONS

A mentor or a leader cannot provide the best advice if they don't know the full story, and a mentee cannot get the help they need without the same. In the context of frankness, the mentor and mentee have to acknowledge that they may have different communication styles that could impact their relationship. For the mentor-mentee relationship to thrive and survive, communication styles that tend toward circumspection or talking around the issue for fear of hurting someone's feelings won't work. Being blunt and direct may be out of a mentor or mentee's comfort zone—or both— but it will be necessary. As a mentor, you don't want the conversation to end up with your mentee leaving the discussion more upset, confused, or adrift than when it started.

No one relishes having a difficult conversation where they need to deliver bad news, provide an unpopular opinion, or recommend something that they know goes against what the person thinks should happen. Mentors and leaders owe it to those who are looking to them for advice to be honest and deliver information unemotionally, clearly, and in a timely manner. Bad news does not get better with time, so you owe it to the individual to initiate that tough conversation and make the message clear. Don't waffle.

There are ways to handle conversations to soften the blow on bad news, but the message should not be delivered in a way that is so nuanced that the key point of the message is lost. What is most important is to make sure the mentee understands the message and has actionable recommendations so they can move forward in a favorable manner or in a way they can understand and accept. Choose your words carefully so that you can deliver the message without crushing them. Pet the cat: Thoughtfully chosen words can get your much-needed message across without having the person become defensive, demoralized, and despondent.

Sometimes these difficult conversations are not planned, due to some specific event or information that has to be relayed. They may evolve from a discussion in which there is disagreement. Remember that there is a difference between not agreeing and not listening. Make sure you are deliberate in communicating that you have heard their side of the story and for areas where you still disagree, why you do. Sometimes you discover that you did not have all of the facts or understand the situation completely enough, and having the conversation allows new information to be presented for inclusion and consideration in the way-ahead decision.

SUPPORT A REALISTIC SELF-IMAGE

There are things you do as a supervisor that you can also do as a mentor. As a direct supervisor, I have found it helpful when going over performance appraisals with a person to ask them beforehand to evaluate themselves and tell me where they think their performance fell on a scale of 1 to 10. I usually see two extremes. When people are asked to critically reflect on their own performance, judged against the criteria for the job rather than their peers, they tend to be more critical than their reviewers might be. Then there are those who think they are knocking it out of the park but aren't. You can run that same drill with a mentee to get them to critically reflect on their own performance and discuss that with you. The first time they hear any negative feedback should not be during an annual performance review with a supervisor, and mentors can and should provide that feedback along the way in addition to what a mentee's supervisors provide.

Some of the hardest conversations you will have as a leader and mentor are with the mediocre performer who views themselves differently. Normally, they are a very hard worker and are ambitious to move up to a more senior position but just don't have the personality, knowledge, skills, ability, or intellect to excel at that level. That is a hard message to deliver without demoralizing the person, but it's your job to do it tactfully. Do not give them false hope or build up unrealistic expectations. Remember, effort does not equal results. Good leaders recognize effort but reward results.

When you have to provide that feedback as a mentor, the best thing to do is help a mentee to understand why they have fallen below expectations and to find the best alternative for them that they would be happy with. When you see they are struggling in a specific situation, job, or even their chosen career field and that it may not be a good fit for them in the end, get them to take the blinders off and look at other opportunities that may be a better fit. They may not have considered these options while they were so laser-focused on their current career path.

Have them work through it by writing down what they value most about their work and what they want to do. Include their goals, values, and career priorities (e.g., continuing to grow and contribute to an organization, build wealth, attain a certain status or position, help others achieve their personal best, continually innovate). Then you can have a discussion with them to remap their path to achieve those same goals through a series of specific prioritized actions that are under their control. Teach them to not let the disappointment of a closed door get in the way of going through an open window.

SIGN OF THE WOLF

As a mentor, you need to be in receive mode before you switch to transmit. As my good friend Captain John Chandler used to say to me, "Barrett, sign of the wolf." What he meant was the classic hand gesture of a canine shadow puppet. It represents having your ears open and your mouth closed.

As they say, seek first to understand, then to be understood. That applies in spades to good communications in mentoring. If you find that your mentee is talking too little, it's probably because you are talking too much or have not given them thought-provoking questions to get after problems. That is ultimately what you want to achieve in your communications: to guide them in finding a good answer, not giving them the answer. How you interact with them in listening to their thought process, as they demonstrate their critical thinking, and eliciting their replies is key to helping them get to the answer.

, Exercising good active listening techniques can help. When your mentee is talking, don't think about what you are going to say next. Concentrate on what they are saying or what they are conveying with their body language. Is there a disconnect between their words and their body language or between their words and their actions? Truly hear what they are saying; don't immediately jump to solving the problem. Repeat back their finer points, then engage them with questions or comments that get them to think through the problem and to consider facts, assumptions, and courses of action that might not have occurred to them yet. In most cases, there is more than one good solution to a problem. Your job is not to tell them what to do; it's to help them see their options and the potential outcomes. Coaching that helps them pick the option that is best for them is the optimal approach.

One-on-one conversations, either in person or virtually via the internet, are important in the mentoring relationship. From the very first meeting, the expectations of communications between the mentor and the mentee should be clearly defined and agreed on. How and how often you will communicate, when you will connect for rudder checks, how you will manage crisis situations that require immediate communication, and how you will agree on transparency and frankness are essential elements in a trusted mentoring relationship. Consider putting together an expectations document, as discussed in Chapter 3, for your mentoring relationship as well.

SEA STORY

A BAG OF BROKEN NOSES

I had a friend that always referred to the contentious, hard conversations as "a bag of broken noses." When you know those conversations are coming, it does not make it any less gut-wrenching or uncomfortable; no one wants to get their nose broken. Regardless, it's your job to lead the discussion with openness and transparency. Don't ever shy away from a tough discussion. Find a way to deliver the message with honesty and empathy. Noses will eventually be reset.

continued

In the Navy, we have selection boards that pick a percentage of people at a certain rank to advance to the next rank. This selection is based on a careful and conscientious review of the person's military performance record. Selection boards are chosen from personnel throughout the Navy to ensure that objectivity and fairness are maintained over time. The officers or enlisted personnel sitting on selection boards understand the gravity of their decisions and know what it means to those they are evaluating. The applicant may be picked to advance, but if not, they may learn that they are at their terminal paygrade.

The more senior the position in the organization the board is selecting for (like master chief, admiral, or captain), the more competitive the boards become. By that time, most of those less competitive personnel have already been weeded out on previous selection boards at lower ranks, so the boards are picking very small numbers out of a pool of rock stars. With the numbers authorized for advancement being restrained by law, the choices for selection boards can be agonizing: A great leader can be passed over due to a slim margin of difference between them and another candidate. The selection boards are tasked to pick the best and fully qualified candidates for advancement. You can do everything right and still not be the right person for selection; you could be fully qualified but not be the *best* qualified.

Selection is based not only on what you have done but also on your potential to do great things at the next rank and beyond. While certain criteria are established in the different career fields and leadership levels to determine which traits, experience, education, and accomplishments will determine what *fully qualified* looks like, the subjectivity and biases of the selection board members also affect the decision.

As all naval officers do, I often mentored those junior to me and took great pleasure in being able to provide guidance and counsel. For those selected for promotion to the next rank, that discussion is normally a happy one and covers their next career steps and the choices that will make them competitive to continue advancing. Those are the easy, pleasant conversations.

But failure can be the elephant in the room that no one wants to address. For those not selected, the conversation is that bag of broken noses. After the selection board results were released, I would reach out to my mentees who hadn't been selected for advancement with a short note to tell them that I understood how disappointing it must have felt to not see their name on the list and that we value their leadership and sacrifices for the Navy. I'd say that if they wanted to talk about their next steps, to call me. While people are normally considered more than once for the promotion (up to three years, in many cases), some may have exhausted their last look and now have different career and life path options they need to consider.

One case was a commander whom I had mentored since she was a lieutenant. Although she was a strong leader with good performance appraisals, she did not make captain. She called me, and I could immediately hear in her voice that she was on the brink of tears and trying to hold it together. I first acknowledged how hard that news must

continued

have been, but as it was her first look, her record would be considered again the next year by a different board; she shouldn't lose hope.

She could not understand why she had not been picked and felt embarrassed at what she perceived as a career failure. Her first words to me were "I did everything I was asked to do, had all the right jobs. Why was I not picked?" The blow was particularly hard because she had expected to see her name on the list. She felt she was in that top 50 percent of the candidates up for selection.

It's hard when you are staring in the eye of the storm to see anything other than destruction, so I needed to help her see what was outside the maelstrom. I did not participate in her selection board, and the rules are very strict that anyone who did participate is rightly forbidden from talking about board deliberations, their choices, or why one person was chosen over another to keep the integrity of the board process sacrosanct. But having participated in previous selection boards, I understood the process and what constitutes a fully qualified candidate, so I asked her to send me her record so I could review it and make comments as if I were a board member. I could identify with specificity where I thought her record was very strong, any areas of concern, and where she might be able to improve and have that considered by a future board.

By objectively reviewing her record against what is considered a fully qualified record, I was able to tell her that she did meet that criteria. Then came the harder discussion, whether her record was both *best* and *fully* qualified.

I was able to show her that while she may have had all the right experience and education and performed well in those areas, there were other candidates that performed better as evidenced by their rankings; her performance appraisals and the recommendations from her evaluators were not in the top category when compared against her peers. For example, although she had been recommended for promotion, she had not been recommended for key leadership positions that she would need to serve in at the next rank. Also, over several years, her recommendations had consistently placed her in the middle of the pack, not in the top 10 percent. So, while she was indeed *fully* qualified, she was not the *best* qualified.

We had a frank discussion about that and about what could be done to change the opinion for the next board and where the horse was out of the barn. For example, a person could not go back and get a new performance appraisal for a job they had six years ago where they received a middle-of-the-road evaluation.

She worked hard on what she could, but during the next two boards, she was not selected for promotion either. The second one was probably harder than the first, as she realized she was probably at her terminal paygrade. After the second board, our conversations shifted to focus more on how she could continue to contribute in the service until her retirement and how to prepare for that transition to the next phase of her life.

In those multiple conversations, she came to see something she perceived as the worst thing that could happen

continued

to her as a blessing in disguise. She had tremendous technical abilities and skills in cybersecurity that were in high demand in the civilian world, and she was excited about the possibilities of using those skills in the commercial world, where she could continue to protect the nation from the other side. She also would have more time with her family and friends, which was important to her.

Sometimes what we perceive as a career failure ends up being the best thing that ever happened to us. It forces us to remove the blinders and see opportunities we would have missed from staying focused on the one thing that we thought we wanted to achieve. It broadens our vision to the possibilities of happiness from other achievements or contributions.

She actually stayed in the Navy longer than she had to, was placed in positions where her leadership was needed, and did tremendous good. Her last job, which she would not have gotten had she been promoted, led to her new civilian career and set her up with the skills she needed to hit the ground running there with immediate success.

THREE POSITIVES

1. Frank and honest feedback between a mentor and their mentee about a career disappointment can lead to seizing opportunities that would have been missed otherwise.

2. My mentee was able to see that critical self-reflection on what our priorities are and why we value them is an ongoing process; life is short, so look for those actions that will bring you the most joy. Don't undervalue or self-limit yourself, or settle.

3. My mentee learned that what may be perceived as career failures can be seen as just bumps in the road, and there is no one path to or definition of success.

+ + +

We define success based on our values and goals, which can change as circumstances, contributing factors, and conditions shift. Our tapestry of a successful life is defined by the people and experiences we weave together, forming an aggregate that is greater than one job or even one career path. The path may not be the straight one we envisioned or the one that brought success for others, but it gets us to the destination that is best for us. As Robert Frost said, "I took the one less traveled by, and that has made all the difference."

FIVE

EFFECTIVE COMMUNICATION

E ffectively communicating their vision and desires to their organization and to those on the outside is one of the most important things a leader can do. Being able to articulate vision, challenges, successes, future plans, and current operations succinctly and in terms that people can understand sounds easy, but it takes time and effort to get right. You need to have a deliberate strategic communications plan that identifies the theme or message you want relayed, the intended audience, the media to be used for information dissemination, the frequency of communications, and the methods of measuring efficacy of the messaging. I normally codify my plan with these specifics, and it becomes a living, breathing document that gets revised for longer-term plans or used as a jumping-off point for similar short-term efforts.

Larger organizations will have public affairs or public relations offices to help with messaging. In smaller organizations, this function is done as a collateral duty, or a staff member may be assigned to speak authoritatively on behalf of the organization. Establish a good relationship with whoever fulfills this role for your organization. They will help you align themes and important messaging that can support your business lines and operations to facilitate communication. They should also monitor news and social media for information about the organization, sharing the status and concerns with leadership and promptly addressing misinformation before it spreads.

INTERNAL VERSUS EXTERNAL COMMUNICATION

Internal communications to the entire organization often take a different tone and tenor than an external communication effort would. When it comes to internal communications, you can speak more freely and focus on specifics to the organization. However, be aware that information you disseminate internally could end up in a broader public forum. While you will be speaking in the family, you cannot assume that that communication will stay in the family. This is especially true of anything you put in electronic format. Assume it will be disseminated to a broader audience than originally intended, perhaps even publicly. Couch your communications in a manner that sets the right tone and gets your theme or message out but would be something that you could live with getting outside the walls of the castle. Sensitive communications broadly sent internally—for example, a company proprietary product or plan—should be clearly labeled as sensitive and any further allowable dissemination instructions defined. This messaging should be part of the overall strategic communications plan as well, for alignment with other efforts and communications so different parts of the organization do not send conflicting signals. Extremely sensitive internal communications should be done in person if feasible.

External communications require an additional level of scrutiny to ensure that the themes and messages will resonate purposefully with the intended audience. Each theme and message, along with the supporting text, should detail and align on the strategic communications plan to specific objectives and desired outcomes. Is the message intended to inform or influence? If it is intended to influence, who is the target, and how have the themes and messages been vetted within the organization and possibly with other key stakeholders to make sure they will meet the mark? Work through possible reactions to the external messaging, and if something is perceived to be contentious or to potentially have a negative impact, determine who may need to know about that prior to its dissemination so they can be ready to stand alongside you in the message. Understand the possible outcomes of the messaging: How will it affect the business and the shareholders, stakeholders, board members, and operations personnel? How will it affect public opinion about the organization, or the organization's reputation, brand, partner collaboration, or relationships involved? Your plan should include prior coordination—time permitting—of your communication with key stakeholders and leadership before the message is released to ensure no one is surprised and also so that they can contribute to it if necessary.

Whether the communication is internal or external, several principles apply. In most cases, messages need to be repeated several times before they sink in, become part of the lexicon, and are widely accepted. Saying something once isn't good enough. Repeat the message using the same language for consistency and to avoid confusion. This reinforces your key points and makes it more likely that the intended effect will be achieved. Words matter, so choose them carefully, particularly for messages that you put out broadly or in the open press. Once it is out, the message lives forever. The first story is normally the one that sticks, so make sure you get it as right as you can on the first try. If that takes an extra day or two, then it is well worth the strategic pause to make sure the message is as accurate as possible and conveys your points in the manner you intend them to be received, embraced, and repeated.

STRUCTURING A MESSAGE: STAY ON POINT

Structuring effective messaging can be a hair-raising task, and you need to consciously endeavor to stay on point. One of the key elements of any good strategic communications plan is investing in the development and distribution of your messages and themes. Critically think through how those communications will be received by the intended audience.

First, identify your intended audience—who you want to influence with your message. The audience can be expansive or precisely targeted to an individual or group. Sometimes you want to reach a broad swath of people; other times you want to find those people who can influence others to take action or positively act on your message themselves. Know who is influential and what their impact is in affecting the behavior of others. Regardless, you should be clear about your intended recipient and why it is important for them to hear your message. Strategic communication is an excellent way to influence both internal and external audiences, but identifying the intended audience is the key to success. You can't hit a target if you don't know what it is.

Next, determine your desired effect or outcome. What—specifically—do you expect to happen when your audience gets your message? If the message is misinterpreted, what will your follow-on action be? Make sure your communications honestly and unambiguously convey what you want your audience to understand. Why does your message matter? Your purpose must be clear, but so must its importance: How does it relate to your business or operational mission and objectives? Does it align with the larger organizational vision and goals? If you need a sense of urgency in the response, make that obvious. All of these are important points to consider with your team in developing your messaging strategy.

Once the theme and message are crafted and the intended audience identified, then you are ready to launch your message. Know your audience and how and where they receive information.

How you deliver your message to them matters. Think about how social media has transformed our culture and how influencers use that platform to their advantage. How did Grumpy Cat become an influencer? Clever marketing, packaging, and messaging, plus a perpetually pissed-off demeanor and endearing sourpuss (pun intended)—who doesn't love that? It's so easy a monkey can do it: There is an entire subculture of vacuous influencers that basically make a living freeloading on social media. Be deliberate about your choice of platform to disseminate your message. If you only use one tool for getting your messages out, you will not be as effective as those with agile plans that incorporate multiple ways to reach a varied audience.

The media used for dissemination depends on several factors beyond the intended audience and their preferences. Consider the frequency of your communication. Too much and people will tune you out as distracting white noise. Too little and your message will not be received or resonate. Speed may also be a factor, in which case social media tools and the internet may be best. Traditional publications, journals, online news outlets, conferences, or professional associations could be other avenues. Your message may be tailored differently for Grandma, who is on Facebook, than it is for your teenager, who is on TikTok (or whatever the hot platform is when you read this). When more precise targeting to a limited audience is needed, that may be done via email, a phone call, or a video teleconference.

Regardless of the media, your team will need to establish metrics for measuring whether the message had the intended effect. This is not always easy, and inundating people with surveys is not the answer. Internet technologies can help to gather data on types of usage on websites, social media platforms, and other web-based dissemination tools, but they will not tell the whole story on how well the message was received. You need to measure not just the output (e.g., a message was viewed by more than a thousand people) but the outcome (those views resulted in a hundred calls to the company about your product or service). So, develop both qualitative and quantitative metrics that can give you a more complete picture.

Identify and leverage communications evangelists and target them in any strategic communication effort. These could be people in your organization or external partners, stakeholders, or others who support what you are trying to do and will help to spread the word on your behalf. Having those with influence help in your messaging can let you quickly reach audiences that you may not have similar access to. Their endorsement also adds to the credibility and viability of your message.

BE AWARE OF SUBTLETY

As a leader, you must also be discerning of the subtle messages you are sending through your words, facial expressions, and body language. Remember, subordinates see and note everything you do, so be deliberate with your words and actions to unambiguously send the message you intend. While carefully chosen words should speak for themselves, we often have a hard time expressing what we really feel in difficult situations for fear of looking weak, uninformed, indecisive, or callous. This frustrates both the leader and the subordinates because neither gets what they want. It can then lead to an ongoing problem of miscommunication or distrust.

Communication failures can manifest themselves not just in what we say but in how we say it. Did we resort to sarcasm, flippant responses, cutting someone off? Body language that is inconsistent with our words is just as harmful; an eye roll, the lemon face, putting up a stop-sign hand, doodling, or playing with a pen can all add "you are boring me to tears" to the message. We have all seen this over the course of our careers; watch out for it and don't do it.

Let's walk through a fictional scenario. You are in a meeting with your cross-functional teams on a big project to discuss an upcoming goal to be met next month. The goal was set several months ago, and the leader assumes that, since there is a detailed plan of action with milestones, everyone is on track and working toward the common objective with speed, resourcefulness, and clarity. As team leaders provide status updates, several briefers talk about unanticipated obstacles that are causing delays. It becomes clear very quickly that the wheels are coming off the wagon and that the objective next month will not be met.

Several of these obstacles being brought to light should have been identified to the group and leadership earlier so they could have intervened and removed barriers to success. They also should have been discussed cross-functionally, and it is evident that they were not or that appropriate action was not taken. The briefing attendees are becoming increasingly uncomfortable, as is evidenced by their body language: shifting in their seats, not making eye contact with leadership, shifting their gaze to those they feel are responsible for the oversight to deflect attention from themselves.

As the senior leader in the room, you are picking up on all of these messages, but also on the subtle shift in the atmosphere in the room. Your reaction will be key to how the situation is ultimately handled and how people present undesirable information in the future. If you react in a way that shuts the briefer down, you have just signaled to everyone in the room that you do not want to hear bad news. And you know what? You won't hear it in the future, leaving problems to fester and worsen, with hugely negative impacts to the organization. However, if you ask thoughtful questions focusing on the team and the problem, not the individual, you will reinforce your expectation for collaboration and working through tough situations together.

For example, you could ask how the team (*we*, not *you*) missed the problem. Is there a gap between the teams that could be closed so this doesn't happen in the future? Was the goal unachievable from the start, and why was that not raised as an issue originally? Did the team have the resources, policies, and procedures in place for success? If not, what needs to be changed, and what are the possible second- and third-order effects of those changes? Do the changes that will result in meeting the goal outweigh the risk of not taking action? What was the delay in reporting the problem, and how can we ensure whatever caused that delay is removed so it is not repeated? Was there or will there be an impact to external stakeholders that needs to be communicated quickly?

A more nuanced approach would be to ferret out whether egos or senior leadership on the team were the problem, in which case changes in leadership may be warranted. That is much more challenging to discover, because direct feedback from the teams is necessary, and there is often fear of reporting or discussing failures of direct supervisors or upper leadership. Again, your reputation for having a willingness to listen and take decisive corrective action and the public perception that you want to hear the unvarnished truth sooner rather than later will go a long way toward maintaining trust and ensuring future situations don't progress to crisis levels.

This is your chance to not be a jerk. You may feel extremely frustrated but take a strategic pause, breathe, and assess your internal monologue a second before you react or speak. If your reaction to bad news involves sarcasm, negative body language (regardless of what you say), a raised voice, or swearing at or talking over the briefer, you will lose your audience. Your words and body language will get in the way of your effectiveness in delivering the message you want. While your message may be spot on, it will be lost in delivery and can be detrimental to how your teams and subordinates communicate with you in the future. You can be direct, and you should be. You can be bold, and you should be. You can be inquisitive, and you should be. You can demand high standards and accountability, and you should. But you can also be kind.

Remember, people don't wake up in the morning and pray, "Please, God, let me be the biggest screwup at work today. I would like to be crowned the new King of Jackassery. Thank you." People want to do well and want to be recognized and rewarded for that. And if they fail or don't measure up to standards, good employees want to know so they can correct their behavior, even though the message may be a hard one to receive. Show them how a failure can be overcome by thinking through a problem and taking corrective action.

CONNECT, CONNECT, CONNECT

Any big muscle movements or actions that could affect the organization should include a deliberate strategic communications strategy. Changes, impacts, and activities can be socialized and shared with key stakeholders, partners, and those internal to the organization. This will help to coalesce objectives and promote better shared awareness and allocation of resources. It will also uncover any disconnection in the organization's alignment between what they say and what they do.

You should aim to stay connected at these different levels in your organization, to rudder check, or to take the pulse of the organization. Small gestures in connecting with your teammates throughout the organization are important. These can be as simple as remembering a birthday, acknowledging that someone has lost a loved one, congratulating them on a promotion or a team on reaching a goal, visiting a sick employee in the hospital, or even something as basic as remembering a name. Leadership at the top, even in large organizations, should still find a few minutes each week to connect virtually or in person with folks in the organization and engage in a conversation. You will be amazed at what you learn about them and what they learn about you.

SEA STORY

STAYING CONNECTED

As commanding officer of the Navy's largest telecommunications station (we had more than two thousand employees at nineteen locations worldwide providing 24-7 communications to deployed forces), I would have my executive assistant schedule thirty minutes twice a week when I would do a walkabout and visit different areas of the main headquarters building just to chat and recognize folks who were doing outstanding work. At first,

continued

this created concern among the mid-level managers, officers, and chiefs, who worried about what the sailors and civilians would say to the direct ear of the commanding officer. I would always share feedback with the entire team on things I heard that we could improve on, and in most cases, people did not use our chat time to air grievances.

We talked about what they were doing outside work that was fun or exciting, what they did last weekend or what vacations they had planned, how their family and children were doing, or what they thought of something that we might be considering implementing that would affect them. When I would first show up in a space unannounced, folks were taken aback and uncomfortable, but after a few minutes of normal chitchat, people were surprisingly open, and our interactions became less awkward or intimidating when they would see me walk by. Respect and protocol were still adhered to, but the discussions had a more general feeling of ease.

I would also reinforce the chain of command. If someone did complain about something, I would make a mental note to address it with their leadership but would also ask the person who they told about it, what they recommended to fix it, and what action was taken. If they told me that they did not address it with their leadership, I would ask them to do that because their leadership would want to know to fix it or help them through the issue. Once a normal conversation started and you listened to what they were saying, it was amazing what you could learn about them and the organization as a whole.

I would also go to the naval hospital to see personnel who were hospitalized, many times for the birth of a baby (we had hundreds of sailors at the command, and many have children while stationed on shore duty), but other times for more serious issues like mental or physical illness. Did it take time to do that? Yes. Was it convenient when I was already working more than a twelve-hour day? No. Did I think it was important that I did it and didn't just delegate it to someone else? Yes! Care for our sailors, officers, chiefs, and civilians extended throughout the chain of command up to me, not just to the first line supervisor. I personally felt it was important to the person to know that and was fundamental to our pledge as leaders to "take care of people." I understand that this becomes more challenging in larger organizations, but you can still make an effort to reach out in different ways, even on a small scale, so you do not create a chasm between yourself and your team no matter how large it is. Gestures don't need to be grand or public to be important.

THREE POSITIVES

1. Getting to know the people who work for you builds trust and reduces barriers.

2. Time engaging with your team is time well spent.

3. Sometimes, the next great idea germinates from a small spontaneous conversation.

SIX

CAREER MAPPING

P assion is one of those terms that generally results in one of two competing reactions. On one hand, you're supposed to be passionate to show that you care about your work and that you're putting serious energy into it. But passion can also be pejorative, implying that you are blind to the reality of a topic or problem. I have often heard that latter meaning throughout my military career: "She is too passionate about this" or "He gets too emotional about that; he is too close to the problem." I never espoused this attitude of dismissal personally; passion is an asset, as long as it goes hand in hand with being able to consider other perspectives objectively as well.

You should be passionate about a topic or problem and should expect the same from others, while making sure that passion doesn't cloud your judgment. You need to be able to look beyond the way you think the situation should go and objectively explore all feasible alternatives. You can then funnel that passion into the right solution.

I find that people who are passionate about a topic or problem bring a higher level of energy and commitment to the project, and when things don't go well, they can get emotional about it. You can help your employees see their way through that by showing them how to apply their passion and energy to solve the problem or get the effort back on track. We are not robots—nor should we be— so you should encourage constructive passion in your organization. Don't be afraid of passion. Instead, embrace it. Use it to solve problems quickly and decisively. As a leader and mentor, you can also connect with the passion of your mentees to help them meet their most important goals in their career and life.

One area that I have always found people are passionate about is in discussing and planning their career. When discussing milestones to be accomplished on the way to achieving career goals, visuals are always helpful. Career maps can help you and your mentee visualize and codify their professional development, their experiences, their education, and other important life factors that can influence their ability to achieve their career objectives.

A good career map is really a holistic life map, because it includes more than just your career. It starts with defining your passion— what brings you joy and what career end you have in mind. For example, you might want to be a CEO, to own your own business, to have a career where you work from home and control your own schedule, to continue to be the best cyber industrial control system expert (or whatever), to be part of a team that is recognized for its continual innovation, and so on. Encourage your mentee to challenge their joy and don't allow them to erect artificial barriers. Have them think about what would bring them the most happiness in an unconstrained way without viewing that through the lens of potential limiters or roadblocks.

Mentors who are in the same organization or industry as the mentee have a leg up to help draw a career map. To be a good mentor, regardless of your specialization, you should connect with someone in the mentee's career field prior to discussing the best courses of action. You should also help your mentee build flexibility into their career path; it can change over time (whether they want it to or not), and you need to leave room for events and passions outside their professional life, such as having children.

When I do career mapping with individuals, I start with where they are now in the journey and get them to talk about what they aspire to do or be. I always challenge them to think bigger, because they sometimes limit themselves on what they think they are capable of but would be surprised at what they can achieve if given the opportunity and resources. People sometimes don't see themselves excelling in a certain role until it is suggested to them, which broadens their perspective on what they could become.

In some cases, they have thought about the "bigger" opportunities and decided those were not for them. For example, I work in technology, and many folks in that field thrive with hands-on technical work and wish to remain in those roles. Moving to higher management levels in the organization might just make them miserable. That is fine. This is about the mentee and their aspirations, not yours. It is your job as the mentor to help them consider options bigger than what they may have thought and let them think through whether those options are right for them. Remember, especially regarding those you mentor in your career field, this is not about making them like you. Your career milestones, experience, and education will certainly shape the advice you give, but there is no one roadway to success; each person's path will vary. So, make sure that you show them how you did it and what other paths to the same or similar end state are possible that may prove to be a better fit for them.

Let's assume that we are doing a career map for someone in the same career field as you. I normally start with an agreed-on end state or objective; in most cases, that goes out fifteen to twenty years. Careers are not jobs; when offering career advice, you need to have the long view. We want to look at what experiences, education, and other factors should be accomplished to make a person competitive or able to achieve their desired end state. What intellectual, skills-based, and experiential tools need to be added iteratively over the years to a person's toolkit to give them what they need for future success?

Using a piece of paper, I start by drawing one horizontal line and add the mentee's current position and their number of years in that field. I also list their significant accomplishments (the positions held, the degrees or certifications they've earned, their promotions, etc.) that build the springboard for the next steps. Then I draw several more horizontal lines to create rows representing points about three to five years apart going up to the twenty-year mark. This gives us a framework to help the mentee determine what specific actions to take and when the best time to do those would be. Timing can be important for specific actions, and as we get to our vertical lines next, we need to be deliberate in understanding where there are timing issues or serial dependencies related to time. For example, your mentee might not be eligible for a crucial position within a certain timeframe if they have not already accomplished other things. Next, we draw three vertical lines to create columns labeled *Career, Life*, and *Collaboration*.

CAREER

The first column, career, starts with the mentee's end state. You then walk the dog back with the mentee and help them list those career milestones, significant job experiences, training, and education that will help them get to the end state on the appropriate timeframe row. I normally break those requirements into two categories on the map: the "have to haves" and the "nice to haves." Those will be determined based on the career path. For example, a "have to have" may be acquiring a certain license or certification in that field before the mentee can move to the next level, whereas a "nice to have" would be a certification that makes them more competitive but that is not an imperative and could be replaced by experience instead. If a specific job is a prerequisite for attaining another job (e.g., if they want to be the vice president for marketing, they will need to have a mid-level marketing job and a degree in marketing first), then those would be have to haves to include in the right timeframes on the map.

Because people often change companies in an industry, you will want to keep the positions or titles specific enough that you and your mentee know (and agree on) what the position entails but vague enough that a different company's naming convention for the position won't cause confusion. If your mentee intends to stay within one organization, then it is easier to be specific and add information about positions, understanding that even those will likely change over time as organizations change. Make sure to note serial dependencies in milestones that the mentee needs to be mindful of. Each career field is different and can be quite specific, which is why if you are mentoring someone outside of your career field, you should have researched the common paths or should agree to include a helpful expert from that field in your career mapping discussion.

LIFE

The second vertical line is a literal lifeline. We often put 100 percent focus into our jobs and the mission of the organization at the expense of all else—our families, friends, health, pets, hobbies, and other passions outside of work. Don't do that, and don't let your mentee do that either. Make sure they are deliberate in their choices for both career and life. Make sure they understand where they can and will make sacrifices in either direction and what the consequences of those decisions may be. Some of those choices may involve professional risk, so be honest about those risks. But also help them put their career and job in perspective with their overall life. A good mentor will provide that kind of holistic advice, guidance, and—often—tough love. As a mentor, you give them things to think about by articulating possible consequences of the choices they will make in the career and life columns of their map.

The life milestones can have serial dependencies too and so should align to the goals and needs of a spouse, child, parent, or significant other as well. While none of this is set in stone, the life objectives provide additional factors for consideration and can affect the career column. With proper forethought and planning, you can help your mentee achieve work–life balance and coordinate important events on their career map.

For example, the goals and success of my family members were of equal importance to my success. My daughter has only wanted to dance her whole life, and she is now a professional ballerina. It was her passion from two and a half years old to today. Knowing that dancing was what brought her joy, I would only take orders to places where I knew she could get her ballet training and pursue her life's passion. It was not always easy. Sometimes we were separated for deployments or other reasons to ensure she could pursue her dream, but it was important that my career did not trump her goals. Getting the mix right required extra planning, coordination, and understanding from all family members.

Another example was my Colombian husband and his desire to finish his college degree. Knowing finishing college was important to him, I worked hard to get orders to a Navy communications station in Puerto Rico, where he could complete his degree in his first language at the University of Puerto Rico, which was much easier than studying complicated medical theories in English.

In both cases, my family's goals were important to them, and what is important to them is important to me. I never wanted them to feel like the things they wanted to accomplish took second place. It took effort, patience, compromise, and understanding, but it was doable. Sometimes it involved taking a different course of action than we originally anticipated, and flexibility was key due to the unpredictability of military life. During times like that, candid conversations with my own mentors helped us work through options that could achieve multiple objectives simultaneously.

Let's say your mentee is a woman and she wants to have a child. When is the best time to do that? She may want children when she is younger, and there are practical considerations, like finances. If she has a career milestone, say, an operational position where she would need to be on call at all hours of the day, that may not be the best time to have a baby. Perhaps she wants to finish her master's degree; it may be helpful for her to take a job where she is exposed to professionals in that field who could help provide advice and act as role models or mentors as she works through her thesis. What if her career requires frequent moves every two or three years like the military? She may want to ensure that her children don't have to move during the critical years of high school and so she would take a position where she is less likely to move during that period. Or say she has elderly parents or a spouse with a significant medical condition. The next two or three years might be a critical period to spend more time with them, and those factors need to be taken into consideration.

Don't let your mentee fool themselves into thinking that everything will just magically fall into place. They need to be deliberate in planning, and that is where you can help.

COLLABORATION

The third line is collaboration. No one travels this journey alone. Many of the best opportunities we obtain are through informal channels resulting from interpersonal networking, teamwork, and relationships. Building a professional reputation takes years and is reflective of the choices made professionally and personally. Collaboration and connecting with others on that journey are important for both what you can contribute and what you can learn. Within that third column, the mentee should list specific actions they can take to expand their network of partnerships, teammates, and mentors at each corresponding timeframe.

Some of the action items in the collaboration column may be to find a mentor who can address specific concerns, such as joining a professional organization recognized by those in their career field, attending a conference and making ten new contacts, writing an article for a professional journal contributing ideas for innovation in their career field, partnering with someone in their field to assist in mentoring more junior personnel, setting up monthly virtual mentoring brown bag sessions, and joining professional social networking channels like LinkedIn and meaningfully contributing to discussions.

Have your mentee build and maintain a database of networks and connections. They should list each relevant person they meet, how they connected to them, and their connection's areas of expertise or importance as a connection. As people become more senior in their careers, it becomes more challenging to keep all of the interpersonal contacts and connections organized, so starting and maintaining a system for doing that early is a good practice. Your mentee can even rate their connections' value based on what the mentee deems most important—for example, a connection provides excellent technical advice, they are well connected in a certain area and can open doors for the mentee, they are a great collaborator and team player who takes action, they go out of their way to lift others up, or they are someone the mentee can help to elevate their game.

Once the career map is done, you should ask your mentee to come back in a week with some specific goals they want to accomplish to achieve the milestones or actions identified in the three columns and for all timeframes. They should have a minimum of three concrete actions (leading with a verb that specifically describes the action) for each column and timeframe, and they should note any required contingencies, dependencies, or serial actions. Also, they should note where they may need help from you or someone else to accomplish the goals.

Once the goals are set, you should check on their progress with a quarterly meetup, virtually or in person. That provides an avenue for ensuring progress has not been lost to the daily grind of work and homelife activities that can distract from achieving long-term objectives. It also provides a more formal rhythm of feedback and discussion between the mentor and the mentee about the objectives

SAMPLE CAREER MAP

◆ Milestone
✓ Education
☐ Experience

TIMING	CAREER — GOAL: VP OF GLOBAL OPERATIONS		LIFE — GOAL: HEALTH AND HAPPINESS, FAMILY/ WORK BALANCE	COLLABORATION — GOAL: REPUTATION FOR GREAT TEAMWORK
	HAVE TO HAVE	NICE TO HAVE		
15–20 Years	◆ Serve as Deputy VP of Global Operations ✓ Complete corporate Executive Leadership Certification ☐ Lead/manage 2,500 people across the globe	☐ Complete 1 month company internship with C-suite leads ✓ Complete external academic Executive Leadership course	– Ensure no moving to maintain stability for husband and kids – Evaluate and implement improvements for long-term mental and physical health	– Volunteer to assist local professional organization to implement programs for junior people – Provide senior mentor advice to 20+ mentees
10–15 Years	◆ Serve as Deputy Major Regional Operations Director ☐ Lead/manage 1,000 people across the Region	✓ Complete Strategic Communications course	– Ensure no moving to maintain stability for husband and kids – Complete NYC or Boston Marathon	– Provide mentoring and leadership training in the org – Mentor 20+
5–10 Years	◆ Selection for Operations Region Branch Chief ✓ Master's Degree in Operations Management ☐ Leadership of watch teams of over 100 people	✓ Complete company finance and budget certification course ✓ Certified Project Management Professional	– Seek assignment in European Region to support husband's career which requires 3-year overseas posting – Travel with family and run marathon in Europe	– "Pay it forward" by mentoring 5-10 people – Publish article and present at industry-related conference
3–5 Years	◆ Complete Watch Supervisor qualifications—12 months ◆ Selection for Operations Division Branch Chief ☐ Regional Watch Supervisor of 50 person team	◆ 2 month internship as Executive Assistant to the VP of Global Ops Region ◆ 2 month internship in another Region	– Have children – Live close enough to take care of disabled parent – Complete full marathon	– Join company "young leaders" group, contribute to monthly meetings – Maintain database of networking connections
1–3 Years	◆ Complete Operations Watch qualifications—24 months ☐ Understanding of operations and customers across regions	✓ Certified in Production and Inventory Management (CPIM)	– Live close enough to take care of disabled parent – Complete four ½ marathons	– Find mentor, meet minimum of 6 x/year – Join the Association of Ops Management (APICS)

and goals and whether they need to be readjusted based on changing circumstances. The career map is a living, breathing roadmap that needs to be reevaluated as time marches on to confirm that it is still meeting the mentee's needs.

SEA STORY

UNDERWEAR EPIC FAIL

Remember: Your career is a lifetime of experiences. Don't let a stumble derail you. Keep things in perspective. As I've noted previously, I am about the most impatient person on the planet, something I would work on more often if I weren't so, well, impatient. It's a cruel irony. Anyway, I was in a rush to go to the bathroom recently and jammed my finger on my underwear elastic so hard that I tore a ligament in my finger and had to wear a splint for six weeks. As my husband likes to note with practically every unimaginably ridiculous move I make, shaking his head in disbelief, "Who does that?" Well, apparently, we have the answer to that burning question. Who learns from that? Hopefully more than just me.

The challenging part of the injury is that I tore the ligament on the tall middle finger—the workhorse for flipping people off in traffic and, of course, on the hand I use for all

continued

of my typing. In a job like mine, where one wields the key-board like Thor wields his hammer, typing with just the four fingers was a new challenge. It was not exactly a can-I-summit-Mount-Everest-without-oxygen-level challenge but a challenge nonetheless.

Wearing this ginormous splint ended up being an unfortunate opportunity to play the movie over and over. I was asked, "What did you do to your finger?" about five times a day. I would have loved a more glamorous story, like I was conducting an offensive cyberattack and suffered a grievous keyboard injury or I broke it in a bar fight over some slight to my awesome husband's character. But no. It was the underwear and my impatience.

So, I told the story, repeatedly, but always with the lesson learned: to just slow down. It would have never happened if I hadn't been rushing. While some may look for blame—like maybe my industrial-strength grannie panties were the culprit—I take full responsibility. Alas, the blame lies only with me and my unending impatience. Most people laughed or sagely nodded and wondered if they would have told a similar story or would have gone with something more generic like "I jammed it," to save public mortification. Even our medical team tried to spare me some executive-level humiliation by putting in my medical record *"She got it caught on her purse."* This actually made me laugh, because it might have been a plausible story to anyone who doesn't know me. Anyone who does knows I am more likely to be found guilty of murder than to carry a purse.

I've always found, though, that the more absurd a story is, the more likely people will remember the lesson. Your career will be long and filled with stories like this; they will not derail your progress. So, go ahead, get over it, and tell that cringeworthy tale. Own it, let someone else learn from it to avoid a misstep, and take away your three positives.

THREE POSITIVES

1. In the case of the underwear, I got a lesson in patience. Just slow down.

2. My brain retrained my other fingers to stop freeloading and pick up the slack for the old middle finger.

3. I learned that my underwear is freakishly strong, like if we ever need an alternative to Fort Knox for storing our national gold reserve, I've got it covered.

A career map is like your underwear. You'll use it both in your career and in your homelife. It hides below all of the other bits you need to function in work or society. And it's not a bad idea to change it periodically.

SEVEN

WORK-LIFE BALANCE

Work-life balance will be as much of a priority as you make it. Allowing your team members time with their families or to take care of their health doesn't take away from productivity or efficiency; it increases it. A proper balance keeps your workforce from burning out, becoming despondent, and leaving. But make sure that your focus on balance is communicated through your actions. Words aren't enough. Many organizations have a mismatch between what they say and what they do. In meetings and official communication, they'll tout their strong support of family and life outside work, then they'll expect their employees to be in the office every weekend or to miss their kid's recital. You've heard that actions speak louder than words, and this is a clear example: What you *do* means more than what you *say*.

The Navy was no different from many other organizations in that respect. For years, I heard comments such as "Your kid didn't come with your seabag" or "You can sleep when you're dead" or "Sure, you can work a half day—twelve hours." While the grim humor was meant to make light of the fact that many folks did not have balance and poured everything into work, it set an unhealthy tone.

In the service, during times of crisis, war, or significant events, giving everything up to and including your life is expected, and no serviceperson would think of doing anything less. It is what we signed up for when we volunteered to serve. All service members know sacrifice is part of service, and we gladly accept that to protect the nation. However, the level of sacrifice during war is different from what you should expect during normal operations. Those behaviors can carry over into the routine business of running the organization, and I have seen many times where false crises were created by leaders who couldn't or wouldn't distinguish the difference and created unrealistic expectations.

Some areas of the Navy were worse than others, and some applauded that lack of balance with an all-encompassing focus on work (which I suppose in some warped way they saw as extreme commitment to the mission). So, it was not uncommon to hear people brag like it was some badge of honor about the amount of leave they had lost, how many deployments they had been on, how many significant family events and holidays they had missed, how many times they could not make a medical appointment or take time for physical readiness training due to work, how they worked thirty hours straight with no sleep, and so on, all in an attempt to impress about their "commitment" to the organization. Being selfless when you are the only person affected is fine. Being selfless at work when you have others who love and depend on you at home can be devastating. You have to carefully manage and balance work and life, or you will be left at the end of the day with nothing but your work. No one strives to have their headstone read "Here lies John. He wished he had spent more time at work."

That sick culture can be insidious if the leadership does not actively promote a different model and work environment. When the leadership positively recognizes that imbalance—or, worse, promotes it—then all the talk about "taking care of people" and "people are our most treasured asset" becomes a farce. You, as a leader, need to ensure that your organizational values are upheld and that the leadership team supports a real work-life balance for your team. There are times of true crisis, when more will be asked of people, and if you have taken care of your people by supporting a healthy work-life balance, then when you need them to go the extra mile, they will be there for you.

Fully committing to an organization includes making sure you are healthy and that the rest of your life is in good working order. It is OK to say no sometimes or to offer alternatives, and you should encourage this on your team. Let's say one of your employees has a cruise planned with their significant other and you need them to attend some training. Their first instinct is likely to cancel their cruise, because they don't want to ruffle feathers, to seem ungrateful or uncommitted, or to create the perception that they are not a team player. Maybe you don't know about the cruise, so the first thing you should do—before assigning the training—is to check the calendar. Does the employee have leave blocked off? If so, respect it and find another time. If not, ask them. It takes only a few seconds to ensure that they have no unannounced plans, and it allows you to connect with them by showing them that their personal life is of real importance. It will also let them know that it's OK for them to tell you when they have plans, even if you forget to ask next time. Now that you've identified the conflict, you should have your employee see if the training is offered at another time or if something similar is offered. Nine times out of ten, it will make no difference to your plans for the organization to reschedule this sort of event.

So, ask the question when you need something for yourself, and encourage your employees to ask for what they need. They are fully aware that any time they ask for a personal allowance, they are taking a professional risk. Make it clear that this is a risk worth taking and that they won't be punished for taking care of themselves. If your organization has a healthy work climate, truly values its employees, and doesn't just pay lip service to the "people are our most important asset" mantra, then you will be open to alternatives that show that you are committed to your people just as they are committed to you.

Making those kinds of choices for yourself—taking your own cruise or keeping that doctor's appointment—also sets a good example for the people who work for you. There has to be a visible connection between your words and actions. Do you practice what you preach when it comes to work-life balance, or do you spout hollow words for effect? When you act in a way that supports your words, your employees see that you have other interests in life besides work that make you whole and feed your overall well-being and that you expect them to do the same. Then you create an environment where you make that happen for them.

In thirty years in the Navy, I never lost a day of leave because I didn't use it prior to it expiring each year. That included being in many tough operational assignments on ships and in Iraq, where it was challenging to find time to take leave. I didn't always get my work-life balance right, and it was certainly not perfect, but it remained a priority not just for me personally but because it set a tone for those I was leading.

Be careful not to send mixed messages and avoid emphasizing through your words and actions that you most value the person who works the maximum number of hours; never leaves the office or takes vacation; eats their breakfast, lunch, and dinner at their desk; and is always on, answering emails and texts after hours, on weekends, on holidays, and at the dinner table—if they are even home then. Value the quality of the work, not the number of hours it takes to do it, and show that you respect those that have balance. It gives the people who work for you the freedom to feel like they can and should do the same and that they should not feel guilty when they choose to prioritize something personal, like a family event, a medical appointment, or attending Comic-Con dressed as a stormtrooper.

While you spend a significant portion of your life at work, it is not the only thing that makes you *you*. Nurture and prioritize those other aspects of your life as much as you prioritize work. Work will take priority over something else at times—just not every time. Achieving a balance is difficult, and you have to acknowledge and recognize competing demands. This is especially challenging when people have complicated personal lives (e.g., single parents, disabilities or illness, taking care of an aging parent, trying to finish their education). If your organization supports you in a healthy and balanced manner, when it does need you to pull the load or go the extra mile, you will do it and they know that. If your organization doesn't support that and you have come to a point in your life where work is the priority every time, all the time, you need to ask yourself why you are working for that organization—and your employees will do the same. Life is about choices, and if you choose to work for an organization with warped values like that, that compromise will result in your paying a high price in terms of personal happiness. Life is too short to always prioritize work above all else.

Be that leader and person who is present no matter where you are and take time off, play, and nurture who you are outside of work. Deliberately carve out time to think for yourself and your team. Have carbon life-form to carbon life-form interactions that feed your soul. Don't joke or brag about a skewed work-life imbalance; brag about getting that balance right and make sure your gravestone does not say "He wished he spent more time at work."

SEA STORY

GETTING SCHOOLED BY A
THREE-YEAR-OLD AT THE HAT PARADE

When I was a lieutenant, I was stationed on a ship in Norfolk, Virginia. I was responsible for the networks and communications services the staff used to conduct operations. My daughter was about three and a half years old at the time and was enrolled in the Child Development Center, a day care facility about five miles away from the ship. I would drop her off in the morning and pick her up at night. She spent a lot of time there, because my normal days on the ship were about ten hours long when there was nothing operationally significant going on; if there was, the days were longer. One time, when I went to pick her up early, she said, "Mommy, what are you doing here? It is not dark yet." Ouch.

I had a lot of mom guilt and felt like I could never get the balance right. I used to try to go to events at the day care when I could break free, like having lunch in her classroom. One day, they were having a hat parade in the morning. The kids each made a goofy-looking hat, usually out of newspapers or papier-mâché, only loosely held together, as most of the glue was eaten instead of applied to the hat. The kids loved it though and took pride in their hats, which they thought looked like some priceless piece of art but more often resembled a dog's breakfast. The level of creativity, intentional or not, on the hats was unmatched even at major art colleges. They resembled everything from a hot dog to something Queen Elizabeth would wear on coronation day without batting an eye. Then there was the one kid with the unintentional Salvador Dalí or Picasso hat—the face with the errant eyeball and out-of-proportion nose that looked like it just got run over by a UPS truck. They would wear the hat on their head and march proudly around the parking lot as a group of impressed parents watched, enthusiastically cheering them on and snapping photos. Normally, the entire event lasted like ten minutes—which, in a three-and-a-half-year-old's mind, made it an all-day event.

So, this one beautiful fall day, my daughter announced on the way into work that it was hat parade day, and she was jazzed. She had the hat of all hats to present at school, clearly a masterpiece, which I had not yet seen. I told her I would be there.

continued

I knew it was going to be a busy day at work, as we had a military exercise starting the following day. The ship was going to be getting underway early the next morning for two weeks, and we were going to have about three hundred extra people joining the staff and all trying to get onto the network accounts to prepare for the exercise. The tricky part about those extra people was that they were not going to be Navy folks accustomed to living and working on the ship. They were going to be people from the other services like the Army and the Air Force. So, there were going to be additional challenges to the normal "help me, my tongue is stuck in the keyboard" type problems the network officer routinely faces. We were going to have a lot of "What's a port? What's a starboard? How do I find my stateroom? Where are the lifeboats? What are all the bells and whistles about? How do I find the ship's list? Whose pants am I wearing?" Anyway, you get the picture. Although I knew we were going to be very busy, I thought I would be able to get out for a few minutes to attend the hat parade without drama.

I dropped her off with a cheery "See you in a few hours," and went to the ship, where I quickly found network chaos reigned—lots of outages and frustrated operators who could not get access to their information on the network and new users who couldn't get their initial access turned on. I kept an eye on the clock, knowing I had to leave about 9:45 a.m. to get to the hat parade on time.

As the clock ticked closer, I got more stressed out. I finally left the ship about 9:55 a.m. and got over to the day care about five minutes after 10:00. The parking lot was empty. I thought maybe they had not started yet and I was still good to go, but no. The kids were on the playground now, wearing their hats and doing that crazy kid run where kids, for no apparent reason, run full throttle in one direction then shift to another direction aimlessly but still at full speed like they are on some special mission.

All except one: my daughter. I saw her across the playground, and she saw me. Have you ever seen pictures taken from satellites where you can actually make out the Grand Canyon or the Great Wall of China from space? That was what my daughter's mouth looked like. At that moment, her face contorted, and her mouth became this big gaping hole. She started to cry and ran over to the fence. My heart sank. I had missed the hat parade.

When she got up near me, she laced her fingers through the fence, reaching out to me on the other side, and said, "Mommy, you promised you would be here, and you weren't."

Epic parent fail. While missing the hat parade may seem like a small thing, it wasn't at that moment to my daughter. She had believed in me and trusted that I would do what I said I would. As I touched her little fingers through the fence, my heart broke. In that instant, I made a decision that I was not going to be "that parent," the one who put work and service above all else, including my daughter and family.

That is not to say that we would not sacrifice over the years or that we would not have challenging times. As a military family, you are faced with separation during deployments, moving every few years, long hours at work,

continued

and always being on call. But by the same token, because it is service and not just a job, we develop a selfless mentality to always do what is asked of us regardless of the price to our loved ones.

I decided in that moment, though, that I was going to get my life in balance and would not prioritize everything else over my daughter.

Fast-forward six months later and almost the same scenario was in play. An exercise was starting the next day, and the ship would be getting underway for six weeks with a couple hundred additional personnel streaming aboard. Communications and network chaos again ruled the day, which stressed out my immediate supervisor, since he was not a communications or network engineer; he was a ship driver who relied on me and the other officers to get the communications right. For those of us who had several years of experience under our belt in this field, we all understood that being a communications officer means never having to say you're welcome, but for my boss, it was new territory, and he was getting heat from his own boss to make sure everyone was up on the networks and preparing for the exercise.

It was my daughter's birthday, and I had cupcakes with melting frosting in the car ready to be presented as a Michelin meal loaded with sugar to a bunch of already hyper three- and four-year-olds at the Child Development Center.

I went to my boss and said, "Sir, I need to leave for an hour to take some cupcakes to my daughter's birthday party at the Child Development Center."

He said, "You can't leave now! It's crazy here with all these people and the problems we are having, and we need to be ready for this exercise."

I told him, "Sir, you are right. It is crazy and hectic now, and it's going to be crazy in an hour and the rest of the day. I am going to be here all night, and we get underway tomorrow. We will get these problems fixed. I just need one hour to do this."

He replied, "OK, but you better be back here in one hour."

So off I scrambled to the center with my lamely decorated cupcakes, which were a hit, as is anything with an overabundance of sugar and neon food coloring with the three- and four-year-old center mafia. But most important, my daughter's face lit up when she saw me, and her faith was restored in my word. She knew how important it was

continued

for me to keep that covenant with her. I was back on the ship in an hour, and all was still chaos, so plenty of job security to go around.

At that moment, I made a choice to do something that was not focused entirely on work. It could have left some to question my loyalty or commitment to the concerns of the organization or the mission. But what it did was make me more grateful that they understood how important that one hour was to my family, and it actually made me want to work harder for the organization. The commitment was mutual and reciprocated.

You need to be savvy enough to know when to play that card. For example, I would never go to the commanding officer of the ship and say, "Gee, I would love to get underway with the ship when we leave port tomorrow, but it's hat parade day at the Child Development Center, so I think I'll take a rain check on that deployment." I also would have explained to my daughter that I wouldn't be there for that hat parade and why if I knew I couldn't make it. And I would make sure I was at the next one when we returned back to port.

What were the professional repercussions of prioritizing my family? Do you think when my selection board for the next higher rank came up that anyone at that board said, "Lieutenant Barrett? Holy cow! I remember she missed one hour of communications checks prior to an exercise back in 1998. There is no way she can be promoted!" Of course that didn't happen. But would my daughter have remembered that I missed her birthday? Absolutely.

THREE POSITIVES

1. Your employers will often let you take care of personal matters, like attending your daughter's school birthday party, if you just ask; and as a leader, be open to similar questions from your team.

2. My daughter knew that day and many subsequent others that she was the priority; she, in turn, supported my career over the years.

3. You can find your balance, the equilibrium that supports both work and life.

I learned early in my career to find a balance between being a good mom, wife, daughter, sister, aunt, and friend and being a good committed naval officer. It wasn't always perfect, but it was my balance. Some people realize that lesson too late, after they have lost connections or burned bridges in relationships with those most important to them. I made peace with myself to live without regret when choosing something other than work as a priority at times. I decided that it was going to be OK in the end, even if those decisions had repercussions to my advancement, which fortunately they did not. There is no replacing years lost and, at the end of the day, as we move on from this life on Earth, you won't wish you worked more; you'll wish you spent your time where it mattered.

EIGHT

FINDING INSPIRATION

A s a mentor, you can help your mentee find the inspiration to excel at what they are passionate about. That can come in many forms—from people, nature, physical objects, music, poetry, and art to acts of courage, grace, and selflessness. I get inspired by innovative, bold thinkers who see a future that others cannot. For me, Walt Disney and Elon Musk are at the top of the list. Who doesn't love a guy who is transforming entire industries—space, automobiles, electrical power—or who looks at swampland in Florida and says, "I see flying elephants that kids can ride on with their parents here"? Then they make those visions into reality. I want to follow those guys.

What I love about Disney and Musk is that they are not just good idea fairies (GIFs)—you know, those tiresome, normally pompous people who love to spout good ideas like they are throwing bananas to monkeys who will just gobble them up and run with them. GIFs normally don't roll up their sleeves and do the hard work to turn good ideas into reality.

Turning an idea into reality is much harder than just coming up with the idea and requires an infinitely large amount of creativity, tenacity, focus, and resourcefulness to do it well. Disney and Musk consistently took their great ideas and put them into action and made them happen. Those are the true geniuses. Did they always get it right? Nope. Both have had (and will have in Musk's case) failures, but they were not deterred by naysayers or failure or those with myopia in seeing the possibilities of what could be.

To keep my inspiration alive and at the forefront of my thoughts, even during the most soul-crushing days of serving in the Pentagon, I had a big picture on my wall of Walt Disney walking under Sleeping Beauty's castle in Disneyland sometime in the late 1950s, after the park first opened. You can find this iconic image through a simple internet search. In the photo, Walt is walking quietly by himself before the park opened for the day and before the crush of kids in cowboy hats and Mickey Mouse ears ran screaming through the park. Then he would have to "be on" as Walt Disney, the icon and celebrity. But in that moment, the camera captured a brilliant man lost in thought. I imagine he was thinking of his next greatest feat of innovation and creativity. His mind was never at rest to what could be. That picture would inspire me and lift me up when I felt beat down by the forces of institutional resistance or inertia, as happens when working in large slow-moving bureaucracies. Having it on my wall also inspired others who would often ask about it, as they were more accustomed to seeing Navy leaders and memorabilia plastered on office walls. It reminded me of the importance of vision, coupled with the hard work of many and tenacity. With that combination, you can make dreams come true, as Walt would say.

Failure can be a springboard for success if we view it that way. Had Disney not failed with Oswald the Lucky Rabbit, he would not have succeeded with Mickey Mouse. Never underestimate the power of tenacity in achievement.

Now that I have left the Navy, the picture of Walt Disney hangs in our dining room, which actually has a Ping-Pong table instead of a dining room table because that is how we roll at our house. The picture inspires me still—and not just to kick my husband's butt at Ping-Pong.

Talk to your mentee about what inspires them and why. Ask them to keep something—a note card, a picture, a screen saver, a talisman—where they can see it to remind themselves to think bigger and to act more boldly than they thought they could. Remind them to not be afraid to take a risk, fail, and take a risk again. Help them inspire others to greatness beyond what they themselves thought they could achieve. Be the person who walks deliberately and confidently into a future that you have crafted, molded, and shaped through your actions, inspiring others to follow.

SEA STORY

SECOND CHANCES

I have had many wonderful bosses over the years who provided, through their example, lessons in leadership that could not be taught in a course or gleaned from a book. Seeing these leaders in action, as well as seeing the say-do alignment of their words with their actions, was inspiring. I learned from our nation's best what it means to be responsible and accountable for taking care of people and critical missions and how to make hard decisions no matter the personal cost. I learned how to admit failure, including personal failure, but also how to fail with grace, pick myself up, and not let a failure become my defining moment. I learned what it means to show courage in the face of adversity, to inspire others through words and actions, to be empathetic to the conditions of others, to think strategically and collaboratively, and to share success and the importance of transparency, integrity, and humility. All of this and more are observed in great leaders and are behaviors future great leaders emulate.

When I speak at a person's retirement ceremony, I often tell them that while the number of years they have served, normally more than twenty, is impressive, it is how they served that matters. They should not judge their success by their terminal paygrade. Rather, it is the sailor they influenced through their actions as a leader that they may not even recall, who recognizes them in a store and comes up to them to say, "You probably don't remember me, but you are the reason I stayed in the Navy," or "You gave me a second chance when no one else would and now I am a chief," or "You inspired me to see that there is no glass ceiling for anyone in the Navy," or "You are the reason I am where I am today." Those are the moments as a leader and mentor that matter. That is the legacy of good mentorship and leadership that is left behind in the end, not a list of professional accomplishments that will be long forgotten.

As commanding officer (CO) of a telecommunications station, I had the privilege and responsibility to take care of our people and ensure the mission was accomplished to the highest standards. With it comes the accountability for everything that happens at the command. There is no sleep for the CO, and it is the ultimate privilege as a leader in the Navy to hold that position. Accountability is absolute in command. As the CO of a ship, for example,

continued

if you are having dinner in the wardroom and your ship runs aground, you are accountable for that, whether you were on the bridge issuing the orders or not. You own it. This is ingrained in the understanding and responsibility of command, and to be in command is what all great Navy leaders aspire to.

At the telecommunications station, we had several hundred people who worked in shifts, or "watches," as we called them. They provided communications and network services to naval forces operating worldwide. While I was CO, we had an incident on watch where several sailors falsified a record of some action taken that carried over several watch sections and involved about ten sailors. Fortunately, their error did not cause an operational problem, but it could have—and a serious one at that. Their error was really one of inattention to detail in the critical recording of events that was not corrected as it should have been by the next watch section. I felt that the most serious aspect of the incident was the fact that it involved an integrity issue, which was of grave concern to me. The sailors involved were mostly young, under twenty-five, and about two-thirds of them were in their first Navy job, and for some, it was their first job ever. I ordered an investigation of the incident to ferret out the facts.

After the investigation substantiated the allocations of misconduct and identified the personnel involved and the cause, I knew that I had to hold those sailors to account. However, I also knew that these were good people who had made an error in judgment that was not a character flaw (something I can't fix) but a mistake that they could recover from. I spoke with my command master chief, who was the senior-most enlisted person at the command, with more than twenty years of leadership experience, and served a special advisory role to the CO, and to my executive officer, the second in command, to get their thoughts about what should be done with the sailors. There was no doubt that these sailors needed to be held accountable for their actions, but at the same time, we also felt that it was a teaching moment that they could learn from and carry forward.

As CO, and under rules that we operate on in the armed forces called the Uniform Code of Military Justice, I had the responsibility to ensure that justice was served and that good order and discipline were maintained. We took those sailors to mast, a formal proceeding in which the sailor is presented the charges against them in front of their CO and other senior leadership. They have a chance to speak directly to the CO, and their chain of command can make comments about the charges and their overall performance. The CO alone, though, ultimately decides whether they believe the offense was committed and then imposes appropriate punishment. A CO has various punishments at their disposal: stripping a sailor of rank, taking away a portion of their pay, confining or restricting them to a certain place for a specified time, requiring them to perform extra duties, issuing adverse letters that become a permanent part of their service record, and so on. In this case, all of the sailors were found guilty of committing the offenses as charged and were punished. However, in

continued

determining their punishment, it was important to recognize that these were good people who made a mistake and
error in judgment that should not be a defining moment for
them. For example, if I had taken away their rank, some
of them would then have had to also leave the Navy. If I
had taken their pay, several of them would have struggled
to support their family; some of them had young children
and didn't have big salaries to start with, so there would
have been additional hardship on them.

I gave them what we call a "suspended bust," where you
take their rank but that punishment is held in abeyance and
only implemented if there is another offense of any kind
in the next six months. I had them perform extra duty in
the form of redoing their watch qualifications and training
others on the procedures they failed to follow themselves. In
the end, all but one sailor remained incident-free, so no one
lost their rank. That one sailor was brought up on a new
charge of misconduct for something else and subsequently
processed out of the Navy.

Standing at attention in a dress uniform in front of
their CO, accused of misconduct, is a painful experience.
All good COs understand the powerful message it sends.
It is not done without deliberate consideration. As CO,
the days I would have to hold mast were my worst in command. However, it was imperative to the good order and
discipline at the command and ensuring that accountability
for actions was maintained. I knew that, for these sailors,
simply going through the CO's mast proceedings was emotionally painful and embarrassing, but it could be an event

in their careers that they could learn and move forward from. Failing with grace knows no rank. It also ensured that the rest of the command understood that we held people accountable for their actions to maintain high standards.

All of these sailors, save one, continued with the Navy—some for their initial commitment only and others for many years afterward. At our command, some had exceptional turnarounds and were recognized later for superior action with awards, medals, promotions, or other accolades for their outstanding work. Several connected with me in later years to say how much they appreciated being given a second chance. One who was later promoted to higher leadership positions wrote me an email to say that the second chance meant the world to him. He said it made him a better leader, better able to deal with adversity, and able to see that true leaders don't support a zero-defect mentality and that part of being a mentor and leader is to help people overcome failure and turn it into something they could then use as a teaching moment for themselves and others. He said it made him think not just in terms of accountability for his own actions but for those of his team and how he now held his subordinates accountable. It helped him understand how measured justice could make a point without killing the career of another future leader.

THREE POSITIVES

1.   The sailors learned that actions have consequences and we have to own the consequences of our actions. Inspiration can even come from perceived failure.

2.   They learned from their actions and, most important, learned that the Navy is not a zero-defect organization, and that we put our trust in good people to learn from their mistakes and to use that learning to make them better leaders in the future.

3.   Second chances can change a person's life for the better in ways they may not even realize at the time; as a mentor, you can help them to see the long view.

+ + +

NINE

PICK THE HILL YOU WANT TO DIE ON

ave you ever worked in an organization where your boss had fifteen number one priorities, and those priorities changed faster than Usain Bolt chasing an ice cream truck? If everything is a priority, then nothing is a priority. Fickle priorities are frustrating for the team, because they cannot ever seem to understand what the ultimate goal is or focus on the most important outcomes. It's frustrating for the boss, because they cannot understand why the organization is not succeeding. This environment screams of indecisive leadership, with the lack of will or understanding on how to strategically look at the landscape of the organization and outside it, put necessary action into context, and appropriately prioritize what matters most.

Sometimes leaders can't see the forest through the trees to properly prioritize so everything becomes a crisis that everyone in the organization tries to respond to. It's like watching 20 five-year-olds chase a soccer ball. In other instances, people feel like they can only act and react if they are in crisis mode, so everything gets prioritized as a crisis. Either way, it is a leadership and management fail.

As a leader, you have to look at the whole ecosystem of the organization and determine what you value and what is most impactful to the mission, customer, and employees. Keep your finger on the pulse of the strategic landscape beyond your organization and how you play in that. As you look for that big picture, which normally involves many complex situations, alignments, and linkages of people, processes, and technology, you will find countless things that are important.

There's an old saying in the military: "Pick the hill you want to die on." It means that you should make a clear decision, focus on achieving that outcome, and then live—or die—with the consequences. You do everything you can to hold that hill—never back down, never give up.

The stakes aren't typically so high in business. You still need decisive action, tenacity, and integrity, and you still need to ensure that your organization and stakeholders know what your priority is and why. By being truly committed to that objective as your priority, you can move forward with purpose, and as the landscape shifts, you can pivot at a moment's notice to keep your organization alive and understanding what matters most. You always need to stay agile and mobile, be ready to reassess whether the hill is worth keeping as circumstances change, and if you see another hill that gives you more of a strategic advantage, by all means, take it. But the organization needs to understand clearly where you have prioritized your efforts and why, and its part in taking the hill.

Pick your hill and charge it. Once you do, focus on actions to accomplish that mission with precision and clarity. Be true to your vision and stay on point. Speak truth to power about what you will and won't be able to accomplish, and make clear what items fall too low on the priority list to be effectively delivered. Good, important, and perhaps otherwise necessary work will get left on the table as it is prioritized lower. You may have the opportunity and capacity to keep those efforts on life support with minimum resources until they become more of a focus, and if you can afford to do that without distraction from the main effort, then do it.

Priorities shift, and good leaders constantly reassess and challenge their previous assumptions to refine where to focus their team's time and energy. Revisit your vision and strategic direction, because things will change rapidly, affected by internal and external influences. Know what the drivers and deliverables are and the right frequency for priority reassessment. By maintaining the pulse on the strategic landscape, you can also help shape it, not just react to it.

ALIGNMENT

Keep your team involved in that prioritization process. They can help evaluate priorities and make sure you have all the relevant facts to make sound decisions quickly. Decide whether an action can be prioritized to be completed in its entirety all at once or whether progress can be shown iteratively to build momentum. You don't need to address everything at once and "boil the ocean."

It can be easy to veer off your hill, to be distracted by something that seems crucial but turns out not to be. This is why careful reanalysis of the driving factors and assumptions is indispensable.

In any organization, a team can easily head in the wrong direction without a strong vision and a consistent and clear focus on what the priorities and goals are from top leadership. More important, as a leader, you must provide the context of why certain priorities matter most. It's not about crafting complicated vision statements; it is about the common understanding of priorities and values and incorporating those in everyday decisions, actions, and results at all levels of the organization. That way, every person on the team can prioritize their efforts aligned to holding the same hill.

THE POWER OF TENACITY

Obstacles may fall—or be thrown—in your path on whatever effort you work on. Being nimble, resourceful, and resolute in your determination to succeed allows you to overcome those obstacles and see them not as roadblocks but merely as bumps in the road. In practical terms, those obstacles come in many forms— people, broken or inefficient processes, limited resources, overly restrictive policies, inefficient or insufficient technology, damaged organizational culture, weak leadership, and so on. Exhibit tenacity in powering through those obstacles. Be imaginative, resourceful, and determined to achieve your desired outcome, even if your path is challenging. When a door closes, look for that open window to go through instead. It may not be how you planned to get to your objective, but you will get there, and in the end, that is what matters. What you learn in the struggle along the way makes you that much more resilient and able to handle temporary setbacks in the future.

Rarely does something go as planned. As Helmuth von Moltke the Elder, chief of staff of the Prussian army, said, "No battle plan survives first contact with the enemy." As a leader, planning for things to not go right and having contingency plans ready leads to success. As a communications officer in the Navy, my job was to make sure that networks and communications systems worked all the time so the commander and the crew could execute their vital missions. Without communications to those higher in the chain of command, other forces we were operating with, and those we were giving orders to, there would be no operations. Due to the fickleness of systems, there was never a guarantee that, just because you planned to use those systems, they would work 100 percent of the time and when you needed them most. I spent a career doing what I called "planning for communications failure." I had the backup to the backup to the backup ready to go at all times. If the primary system didn't work, we instantly jumped to the secondary or tertiary system and were back off to the races.

When the pressure is on, everyone depends on you and your team to get it right. Being a communications officer, like all service providers, is a thankless profession. It's a given that you will be ribbed by your shipmates for never fully meeting everyone's expectations or being at the top of the food chain (I can't tell you how many times I heard "What are the three best years of a communications officer's life? Second grade . . . " followed by raucous laughter). You are already working against a perception that you are a drooling mouth breather with your tongue stuck in the keyboard if things don't work 100 percent of the time. Don't pay attention to perceptions like this; let them go like water off a duck's back. Focus on meeting your mission. Being in that kind of high-stress environment with many contributing factors that are beyond your control forces you to be tenacious and resourceful to get that mission done.

Being tenacious does not mean that you ignore the warning signs that you are on the wrong path. Something you think is the answer may be superseded by other options or solutions. You don't want to fall victim to being too stubborn to realize that you have made a mistake and are bumbling in the wrong direction. Critically look at obstacles and see if they are ones you need to leap over or go around or if you need to change course. Take the blinders off and constantly scan the horizon for what makes sense in a changing landscape. You may have to make minor—or major—adjustments on the path to the final objective, but that is fine; there is hardly ever just one way to achieve a goal.

On a personal note, there will be many times over the course of your career that what you think will happen or what you wish to happen doesn't happen the way you thought it would. Those career disappointments can feel devastating at the moment, but by putting on your tenacity big-kid pants and digging in like a tick to find another path to go down, it will lead to success in the end. Your path may not be that clean straight line that you envisioned. It may require extra time, work, and effort to achieve your goal, and that is OK. What you learn along that path shows your tenacity to overcome obstacles and how you stick with a challenge until you overcome those obstacles. It will earn you a reputation for hard work and as someone who gets results and will serve you better than if success had been handed to you.

INTEGRITY

There are some businesses where the corporate culture does not place a priority on trust or integrity. This will be clear through which employee actions are tolerated. While the organization's mission and vision statements may tout exceptional values, in practice, they are not enforced. The worst environment is when behaviors that run contrary to the stated values are implicitly rewarded or when management turns a blind eye and allows them to persist, where loyalty and comradery are not valued.

This is completely foreign to me. In the military, everyone looks out for each other like a family. We leave no one behind. Friends who have made the transition from the military to civilian organizations have been appalled by the lack of integrity and loyalty that existed in certain companies. If that is the corporate culture where you are and it is untenable for you, you need to ask yourself why you still work there. If you are the leader at an organization like this, you need to ask yourself three questions: How did you let your culture move so far from your ideals? And why would your employees stay in a place like this? What needs to change?

There will always be another job where you don't have to support that caustic culture. Do not let a culture like that change who you are or what you stand for. Your moral compass and values are the hallmarks of your leadership and reputation, so don't squander them by accepting less or allowing the bar to be lowered.

Remember: Life is short. You don't have to work for or with jerks. That is a choice, so choose not to, because there are enough people who won't act that way and will appreciate that you don't either. Be clear on your standards, then stick to them consistently, publicly, and with transparency in your communications and, more important, in your demonstrated actions.

SEA STORY

YOU KNOW WHAT THEY CALL THE PERSON WHO GRADUATED NEAR THE BOTTOM OF THEIR OFFICER TRAINING CLASS? ADMIRAL.

I went to college in Boston, and my family did not have a lot of money, so as with most Americans, it was a struggle to figure out how I was going to pay for school. My parents were able to help a little, but tuition was expensive, and being creative and resourceful about how to pay it was top of my list.

I wanted to attend a certain college and told my parents I wasn't going to go to the state school where I grew up beyond one semester, and that if I had to quit school to earn the money to go where I wanted, that is what I was going to do. So, by January of my freshman year, I found myself at an expensive private school in Boston with a partial scholarship, a little help from Mom and Dad, two part-time jobs, and a full course load.

I knew I wanted to be a naval officer, and I also knew that the Naval Reserve Officers Training Corps (NROTC) offered scholarships for full tuition and books. When I went into the NROTC unit to discuss how I might be considered for a scholarship and how to join their officer training program, they said that to be considered for a scholarship, I would have to take calculus and physics.

Now, as we've already established, I don't do public math; it is not my thing. My brain immediately went into overdrive to find another means to an end. Be tenacious, I told myself, and don't be deterred. I knew that I needed to maintain a certain grade point average to retain my partial university scholarship and that if I took calculus and physics, not only would that grade point average most likely drop, putting that scholarship at risk, but it would be highly unlikely that I would have sufficiently high enough grades to get the NROTC scholarship. Being pragmatic about that, I asked if there was any other way that I could participate in the training—if I could do everything that all of the paid NROTC students did

continued

but without the financial support from the Navy and get my commission as an officer at the end. They agreed that I could do that, so I was off to the races . . . sort of.

First, I had to figure out how I was going to continue to pay for school beyond that first semester. I quickly found a company that placed students in local homes as nannies, babysitting and doing light housework in exchange for room and board. I found a wonderful family that I remain close with to this day; they are my second family. I lived with them for more than three years, and they were generous enough to let me stay long beyond when they needed me, as in the kindness of their hearts, they knew I needed them. I am forever indebted to them and cherish their friendship. Second, I found a job managing a café for several hours every day and on the weekends and took out student loans, which I paid for over ten years.

Three years later, taking a full course load, plus extra NROTC drills and classes, and working two jobs, I received my commission aboard the USS *Constitution* in Boston Harbor as an ensign in the US Navy. Mission accomplished. And I escaped the evil twins of calculus and physics. Not today, Satan. Not today.

One day during my time at the university, however, I was called into the NROTC unit and was given a dressing down. I was pulling a C- in my naval engineering class (no big surprise there) and needed to manage my time better to study more for that class. I sat there listening to the lecturing lieutenant with a bit of angst, not for my grade (because, frankly, a C- in naval engineering would have made it on the fridge door of academic excellence with a big fat gold star in my house), but with my mind racing about how I was going to get across Kenmore Square in the next five minutes so I would not be late for my second job. So, I asked him politely to speed up the time management lecture so I could get to work. Ah, the irony.

I also learned much later, as I crossed paths with officers who had been our instructors and leaders at the NROTC unit, that everyone was pulling for me and helping behind the scenes because they knew how hard I was working. They would discuss who was going to give me extra instruction in celestial navigation or naval engineering that week or who was going to check up on me to make sure I had my uniform right. These great mentors quietly and graciously snowplowed obstacles from my path, unknown to me.

Was I resentful of other students that had full scholarships? No, good for them. I'm happy if anyone gets a good deal. I was just grateful that I could find a path to get to the same end state too, albeit a circuitous one.

What I learned in having to work harder during those years than my peers at the NROTC unit who were on full scholarship was indispensable to the work I later did in the Navy. I learned to be tenacious and resourceful and to multitask and manage time. At the end of the day, it doesn't matter if you have to do something more or something different from someone else. Keep your focus on your goal. Don't give up, and you will get there. The journey you take will have value that you sometimes cannot appreciate in the

continued

moment, but it carries you through other situations in life. And it helps you better lead others to do the same, which you may not have been prepared for otherwise.

THREE POSITIVES

1. I learned incredibly valuable skills during my time at university and in the NROTC: tenacity, resourcefulness, multitasking, and time management.

2. I made lifelong friends with people I lived with and worked with as a result of not having an NROTC scholarship that I value more than my naval career; they are an irreplaceable gift in my life and I could not imagine going through the last thirty years without them.

3. I graduated at just about the bottom of my NROTC class, but I graduated.

A bonus positive for counseling Gen Z members or Zoomers: Calculus and physics are for chumps. Take Geology 101 ("Rocks for Jocks") as your mandatory science course. You can learn critical thinking skills elsewhere.

Nothing replaces tenacity in achieving goals. You learn more having to work a bit harder or differently than expected. The value of those life lessons is incalculable and often repeatable in other situations. And the result is what matters in the end. You know what they call the guy who graduates at the bottom of his medical school class? Doctor. You know what they call the gal who graduates at the bottom of her NROTC class thirty years later? Admiral. Mic drop. Don't ever give up.

TEN

LEADERSHIP AND MENTORING IN TIMES OF CRISIS

Y our organization will experience a crisis at some point. It may be temporary, or it could be existential. Either way, the crisis is real, and how you respond sets the tone for how you will come out of the crisis at the other end.

If you have established a reputation as a person of courage, integrity, intelligence, empathy, good judgment, and transparency, then your employees will be with you from the start, supporting what you ask them to do. Those requests may be above and beyond what they have normally done; testing the status quo in challenging times is expected.

If you haven't built that reputation, you face an uphill battle, particularly if your deficiencies lie in a lack of transparency and integrity. Those are character flaws not likely to be corrected; rather, they are exacerbated in times of crisis. Having a slow and steady hand during a crisis is imperative, as is being inclusive by surrounding your organization with experts, or the best minds to collaborate with on solutions and recommendations for the way ahead. This will not just get you through; it could be transformational in ways that were unimaginable before the crisis. Never let a good crisis go to waste. Find the silver lining that helps your organization come out better in the end.

The coronavirus (COVID-19) pandemic of 2020 is a perfect example, a seminal event in the lives of everyone throughout the world. The speed at which the virus spread and changed daily life for all Americans was the stuff of movies. While experts had foretold the potential catastrophe of a pandemic, most American leaders didn't have a planned response when it happened. This, coupled with disinformation fueled by social media, caused more chaos.

Take toilet paper, for example. When Americans thought they could not get access to toilet paper, they bought and hoarded it, whereas if people had continued buying at the normal rate, everyone would have been fine. The solution was clean and simple—literally. But that is not what happened. Making matters worse, there were "meet me in the Octagon"–level brawls at supermarkets for packages of toilet paper, hand sanitizer, and beer (OK, depending where you live, that last one could be a normal Friday night). Good people behaving badly became a national shame.

Now, I am not a fan of the "just in time" toilet paper supply theory, especially on taco night (although my dad, who lives in and proudly reigns over the Kingdom of Bad Dad Jokes, would say "that depends"). Having a few extra rolls around is normal; having a hundred is not, unless you are going to toilet paper your neighbor's house (which, by the way, during the pandemic would have significantly increased their property value, so you would have actually been doing them a favor). But fear drives people to behave in irrational ways.

This kind of irrational behavior will happen during a crisis at work too, which is why leaders and mentors need to expect a crisis and plan for it. You must be preemptive in addressing it and assuaging angst. You need to demonstrate measured, rational thinking and communicate it in a manner that addresses the fears and uncertainty in the workplace. Your people will be looking to you for the plan that addresses what matters and their fears of the unknown or turmoil. When you don't have an answer—particularly for things out of your control (e.g., how fast the virus was spreading, how long we would be shut down), you need to be honest and crystal clear about that. Take decisive action on that which is under your control and communicate what you are doing, as well as the objectives and the possible second- and third-order effects of the action, and execute. Also be clear about what you cannot do. Acknowledge it and make sure the team understands your limitations in doing something about it. If time is of the essence, then communicate that to employees quickly, so they understand their part and the sense of urgency necessary for success.

PLANNING

When a crisis occurs, articulate clearly your way ahead early in the response. Don't wait until the horse is out of the barn. If there is something that you didn't do to prepare, you have to seize the moment, recognize the shortfall, and quickly implement plans to overcome it. These plans need to address the organization's "no fail" missions and care for employees. Gather a small team of experts on the business, people, stakeholders, infrastructure, and company policies or procedures. Take no more than one or two days to come up with a plan, including the relevant strategic communications, and start executing it within forty-eight hours.

That small crisis action planning team needs to be collaborative and diverse in its thinking and in challenging the status quo so you don't fall prey to groupthink. Planning must start with the known facts and assumptions and having confidence in those (Where did the fact or assumption come from? Is it essential to the planning to continue, or is it a distractor? Is the information time-sensitive, or could it change rapidly, thus changing the plan?). Determine which tasks and subtasks are needed, when those are due, and who would execute them. Clarify task dependencies that have to be put into a timeline to ensure there are no gaps that could derail the plan's courses of action. What strategic communications must accompany the plan to inform the broader audience, internal and external, of what is being done, why, and by whom?

Planning also needs to include the what-if factor. In the Navy, we called this "war gaming." You take your plan and run it through the intellectual rigor of asking, "OK, if we do this, and that happens, how will we respond? Can the original plan stand, or will it change?" This includes thinking through second- and third-order effects, looking for unintended consequences that may cause problems later. The plan may only be 60 percent accurate based on known facts at the time, but it will be the framework for future action. Get this team together every few days after the plan is promulgated to reevaluate assumptions, as new facts may rapidly change courses of action, and the strategic communications themes and messages to be put out. Strategic communication becomes vitally important to frequently—in some cases, daily—reassure customers, employees, and stakeholders that the organization is acting with resiliency, deliberately and effectively continuing its "no fail" missions.

A well-thought-out and fact-based plan is always necessary, but even more so in a time of crisis, when people will look to leadership and mentors for guidance and hope. It's not the time to shoot from the hip and rely on chicken bones and voodoo. We often joke in the military that "hope is not a course of action," and while that is true, it is still an essential part of any plan, particularly when presented with no good options. The leadership team's ability to convey the plan in a positive way and to offer hope for success in uncertain times is important. That is not to say that we should allow ourselves to be blinded by reliable information that may run counter to what we believe is happening or should happen. We need to be open and agile enough to change the plan as circumstances and new information are obtained.

MEASURING SUCCESS

You should establish a set of metrics that will allow you to know whether you are getting the response right. These can be internal (Did we continue to produce X number of widgets a day?) or external (Did our customers understand why there was a delay in processing their product?) as well as both quantitative and qualitative. Spend some time at the beginning of a crisis to define what success will look like and how you will measure it. And during the plan's execution, you should also reevaluate your metrics to validate whether you are using the right ones and measuring well.

If the plan goes awry, go back and analyze why. Double-check the incoming facts and assumptions and what may have changed due to external influences during the course of the plan execution that was unexpected or impactful. Then adjust course as quickly as possible. Ask how you and your team are checking the pulse of factors that are influencing the crisis. How does that affect your plan to continue to execute your "no fail" mission? When things don't go as planned, communicating the misstep and what is being done to correct it quickly and clearly will maintain higher organizational confidence in your leadership and your ability to steer the ship through the storm with the support of the entire crew.

CLEAR COMMUNICATION

Frequent, factual, and transparent communication during a crisis is critical. Leaders must project strength, confidence, and hope but also acknowledge uncertainty, concerns, fear, angst, and anger and address those factors head-on. Be open to dialogue and address issues from employees swiftly and frequently. You can do this in a number of ways, such as a virtual town hall meeting. Rumors can start and spread quickly, and your open and frequent communication and willingness to address misinformation or concerns right away will quell much debate. As a leader, you don't need to justify your actions, but I have found that providing context for decisions, particularly those that will be unpopular but necessary, is extremely effective. People will be much more apt to follow your lead if they understand the bigger picture, that your commitment to the organization and to them remains the highest priority, and what their specific supporting role is. Visibly show strong leadership when unpopular decisions or conversations are needed.

The crisis may be extended, and you and your leadership team should communicate that difficult message as well. You should set an end state goal, even though the end state date may be unknown. As leaders and mentors, we work with those in the organization to reach that goal and to express that everyone has a critical part to play in its success. They all have control and ownership in shaping the end state, and it won't be possible without their contributions.

People are inherently good, aside from toilet paper hoarders and those that drive too slow in the left lane, so find the good and celebrate it during a crisis. It doesn't take much effort for a senior leader to make it known they want to hear of the extraordinary efforts people are putting into the mission and in helping their teammates during a crisis and to act on that information. Specifically ask for that information daily and make it a point to recognize people and teams publicly. Lionize good behavior. Find the good and celebrate it often as a reflection of the organization's values and the incredible commitment to outstanding employees that the organization appreciates. Sometimes, something as simple as walking by a worker's desk and stopping to say how much you appreciate a specific action they took makes a world of difference. Make it your job to ensure your employees know they are special and appreciated.

OPPORTUNITY AND INNOVATION

Look for the unexpected opportunity to come out of a crisis. What is it that we can change or transform in the organization that will make us better leaders, partners, teammates, stakeholders, and a better organization as a whole? What can we seize on that may be an opportunity to quickly remove long-standing barriers that could be transformational? Again, we can look to COVID-19 for an example of this in the shift to working from home for many white-collar jobs.

Prior to COVID-19, many industries aside from technology firms, including education, academia, small business, and retail, were lagging or uninterested in shifting their business and process functions outside traditional brick-and-mortar settings to allow remote work. During COVID-19, whole industries across the world shut down their in-person transactions and implemented social distancing in hopes of slowing the virus spread. They quickly turned to look at what work they could have their employees do from home. This would keep the employees, customers, partners, and coworkers safer than interacting in person. Many organizations started thinking about how they could operate this way after the horse was already out of the barn and their physical businesses or schools had shut down. They had to play catch-up with information technology infrastructure, policy, training, and procedures, which resulted in bumpy starts and lost productivity.

Even with all the bumps and bruises along the way, the result is that we are likely to see a societal digital transformation of how effective work is perceived. What will this mean for your organization, and how can you see it as an opportunity rather than a negative? Trust can be a concern for management in a remote work environment, particularly for those that did not grow up as digital natives. The old mistrust of telework surfaces: "I can't see the person, so how do I know they are not taking a bubble bath, cleaning lint out of their belly button to knit a sweater, or watching *Gilligan's Island* reruns?" However, if you don't trust your employees to work from home, you probably don't trust them in the office either and are just not admitting that to yourself. Trust issues need to be addressed, regardless of where your employees work.

Discover the opportunity in chaos. Leaders should put aside their fears and see this digital transformation as an opportunity for their business to improve, grow, and attract even more business and higher-quality workers. There will always be some work that cannot be done from home because it requires a physical presence (e.g., working on classified information for the government), but much can be done with improvements in cybersecurity, networking, and information technology. Is it perfect? No, but neither is working in a physical building. There are just different challenges to address by managing expectations, setting clear work outcome objectives, and ensuring employees have the capability, tools, and training to perform, collaborate, and communicate securely. Some people, particularly extroverts (you know Chatty Kathy, who swings by your desk to talk about the recent family reunion that reinforced her notion that they had no lifeguard at their gene pool?), may not enjoy working from home, so there may be ways to improve their collaboration online to replicate the casual pickup conversations at the office or to introduce a hybrid model, where some personnel remain in the office and some work completely remotely.

An example of developing a hybrid work structure might be our crisis action planning team's initial planning efforts. The preferred method might be to have the team in one room as much as possible for the short sprint planning, with only those unable to be there in person joining in remotely. That might speed up progress in getting to viable recommendations and solutions more quickly and in avoiding possible technology-induced disruptions. But if that is not possible, those sessions would have to be remote, via web conferencing, and you would have to figure out how to achieve similar results as efficiently as possible.

The general societal impacts of allowing remote work are exceptional. You can attract talent from all over the world that you might not have had access to before. It reduces pollution because fewer commuters are on the road (we saw this in satellite imagery of major urban areas during the COVID-19 shutdowns), and employees appreciate not wasting time and money sitting in traffic. There is less need for large office buildings, reducing your overhead. The technological improvements to support changed work processes, such as better information technology, tools, and cybersecurity capabilities for remote workers, improved the infrastructure to support the bandwidth demands even in isolated areas.

And the benefits to employees have proved plentiful. Working remotely enables more time with family, friends, and pursuing passions. Time not spent commuting is time lived well doing other things. Child or elder care can be better managed, and there are more opportunities for employees with disabilities and limited mobility. In a study by Pennsylvania State University, employees reported that while working remotely, they were more productive, wasted less time, were better able to manage a work-life balance, and had improved work relationships when communication was strong.[1]

---

1 "Telecommuting a win-win for employers and employees," Penn State News (blog), December 3, 2007, https://news.psu.edu/story/192069/2007/12/03/telecommuting-win-win-employers-and-employees.

Another example of opportunity and innovation out of COVID-19 was in something as simple as recipes. My daughter Face-Timed me about five days into their citywide quarantine and showed me the ingredients she had in her fridge: a potato that looked more like a science project than something you would actually eat, garlic, half a red pepper, some tofu, a partial red onion, and a package of mushrooms shockingly lacking the mold for which her refrigerator usually wins Michelin stars. We came up with an emergency stir-fry recipe with the help of a mixed bag of rice and some sauce. In doing so, we discovered several websites that had popped up since the pandemic had started that help starving Millennials through such circumstances. You can go to the site, enter the random items of what-might-otherwise-be-known-as-food-if-it-was-not-so-old, and the site provides you recipes. Bam! My kid was off to the races. So now when you are in quarantine with a jar of salsa, two beers, left-over pink Peeps from Easter, moldy cheese, and four thousand rolls of toilet paper, you will not starve. There is hope.

To further enhance the positive outcomes of the coronavirus pandemic, I'm including an extra set of three positives. COVID-19 is still in full swing as I write this. Much of the crisis—especially the tragic loss of life—may have been avoidable if we as a nation had a better pandemic response plan. As leaders, we need to analyze our organizational lessons learned and make decisions about changes that should be permanent and forward-leaning. Inevitably, some other seminal event that will disrupt our lives (like 9/11, Hurricane Katrina, the coronavirus) will happen again. We need to ensure our resilience to fight through the hurt and take care of each other. This will be the hallmark of our success.

THREE POSITIVES

1. People went to extraordinary lengths to put others before themselves.

2. We were forced to innovate.

3. Just-in-time toilet paper is not a good idea unless you plan to load up on the cheese intake.

+ + +

COVID-19 forced us to transform our thinking about what work looks like. This produced creative options for additional goods and services. From K–12 and college education to grocery and restaurant services, every segment of the economy (business, health care, agriculture, transportation, energy, the arts) has been affected. Many of the changed processes and policies and new products or services will endure long after COVID-19 subsides, making us a nation of innovators and better for it.

Good was everywhere during the pandemic, from selfless health-care workers, first responders, the military, and grocery store workers to average citizens who shared food and supplies and lent their time and talents to help others. The pandemic enabled a whole nation to reconnect with their families. Board games were brought out, people went outdoors to hike and play, and more concern was shown for family—particularly for teaching younger generations the importance of social responsibility for the elderly and infirm. My hope is that these behaviors will continue long after the movement restrictions implemented to prevent the virus's spread are relaxed.

SEA STORY

WHAT ELSE DOES SHE NOT KNOW?

My first position as an admiral was a high-stress job where we were responsible for military cyber operations across the globe. I was in charge of current operations, so any crisis that was happening in real time fell in my wheelhouse. While I had a lot of experience in cyber defensive operations and information technology, I was new to some of the intelligence aspects of the job and had a steep learning curve coming in. I was reading a lot, studying up on what I didn't know, and relying on subject matter experts who had been doing cyber intelligence for years to help me learn.

One of the daily events that I was responsible for was a morning brief I would hold on behalf of my boss. During this brief, all of the key watch centers and personnel around the globe would connect, and we would discuss current crises, go over the current state of the Department of Defense networks, address concerns, and prioritize and synchronize efforts on cyber operations. Normally, there were about a hundred people on the watch floor where we held the brief and several hundred more at other locations who attended via video teleconference. One morning, after I had been in

continued

the job for about a month, we were being briefed on some adversary cyber activity, and I had a question.

In the military, operations and activities are often given code names to identify them more simply. They are often ridiculously named things like "Stinky Pumpkin," and there are thousands of them. During this particular brief, someone was discussing an event using a code name I was not familiar with, so I asked the briefer, "I am not familiar with the nation-state associated with that. Who is that?" The briefer provided the name of the malicious cyber actor behind the incident, and I thanked him.

Two seconds later, before the briefer resumed his presentation, someone on the video teleconference said clearly and for all to hear, "She doesn't know that? What else does she not know?"

Cue awkward silence.

Now I realized in that moment, which was professionally embarrassing, that I had a split second to decide how I was going to react to that comment. This was a mini personal crisis. I could go full-on *Game of Thrones* or make it a teaching moment about confidence and humility in leadership.

So, I yelled, "SLAAAAAYYYYYYY HIM!"

No, what I actually said to the whole group was "Listen, I am new to this job. There are a lot of things that I don't know, but you do. We are a team, and I am relying on you as the experts to help teach me those things I don't know. And you have an open microphone, shipmate." Everyone started laughing, easing the tension of the moment.

Was that humiliating for me? Sure. Especially being as

senior an officer as I was. Was it a movie I was going to play over in my head again and again, causing me to doubt my self-confidence? Nope. It made me more determined to learn more, faster. Three years on, no one would even remember that incident. It didn't and doesn't matter. But it was a teaching moment for everyone in the room about having the confidence as a senior leader to admit you don't know something and the humility to accept help, particularly in times of crisis, that others do know, and that you need them as part of a team effort to be the best collectively. Remember, it's not about you and your ego.

This is true in any crisis: You need to have a plan, trust your team, communicate clearly, and be prepared to learn.

THREE POSITIVES

1. I asked for help when I needed it rather than feigning my way through the briefing—which could have had disastrous results.

2. I made a split-second decision and lived with the consequences.

3. Ironically, the following week, my boss was at the brief, and he asked the same question about another incident; thankfully, all the microphones were muted that time.

+ + +

What was most important to me in that moment was how to show that a leader should be confident and comfortable to not pretend to be the smartest person in the room. Asking for help when you need it is a sign of strong leadership and should be encouraged at all levels of the organization.

Sometimes you have only a split second to react in a situation. Your confidence in yourself and your team and your ability to think on your feet to provide the right guidance to move ahead or diffuse the situation will instill confidence in your subordinates. When crises arise, they know they will be able to rely on your good judgment and leadership to get you all through it together.

ELEVEN

FAIL WITH GRACE

Having been in leadership positions for the past thirty years, I've earned my share of battle scars for screwing things up. You don't know what you don't know, or sometimes you just make the wrong choice, even with the best information, intentions, and support from your team or senior management. But there are very few mistakes that you cannot recover from with the right degree of humility, a proactive demonstration that you've learned from it, and confidence in yourself and your core values to right the wrong.

Do not let others cause you to doubt that last one. Your confidence and the confidence you instill in others with your integrity, reliability, transparency, steady hand, vision, and uncompromising standards will have people continuing to line up behind you, wanting to work with you, and continuing to support you even through failure or missteps. It also teaches those junior to you that there is no such thing as a zero-defect mentality in your organization.

Everyone—even senior leadership—is accountable and must take responsibility when things do not go well, learn from it, and move forward with a better plan for success.

ACCEPT THE FAILURE

Accepting failure means accepting risk, and organizations need to understand and communicate clearly what their tolerance for risk is to their core missions. No great reward was ever achieved without some degree of risk. To encourage calculated risk-taking, your team needs to know that it will be OK if they fail at times in striving for that objective. That needs to be demonstrated in both words and actions by leadership in support of their efforts at excellence.

If something goes awry, take the high road and fail with grace: Admit mistakes when you make them, and own them. Be humble about learning from a mistake, and then move on. Don't dwell on it. It's in your rearview mirror; you can't change it, and it will only cause you self-doubt if you play that movie in your head again and again. Move on with confidence and never let a failure define you. Let it only increase your resolve to succeed next time, and let the failure force you to look at the opportunity you would not have even seen had the other door not closed. My biggest professional failures ended up being the best things that ever happened to me, although at the time they felt demoralizing, embarrassing, and devastating and forced me out of my comfort zone.

Don't be too hard on yourself or overly critical of your subordinates. I know and have worked with a lot of Type A's over the years—hardworking, self-sacrificing, focused, smart, top-of-their-game performers with eye-watering achievements.

They also tended to be perfectionists and beat themselves up over little details. Be OK with celebrating the gaffes and accepting failure in yourself and others.

Demonstrating that you can fail with grace is important as a leader. We tend to amplify the importance or impact of our actions, but unless someone is going to die, it's probably not as bad as it seems. Sometimes the best thing that can happen to you is failure. It makes you resilient, resourceful, more understanding, and better able to tolerate failure in others. It shows your vulnerability, humanity, that you are not infallible, that failure doesn't deter you from doing, saying, or being the right thing in the end. You can recover from failure. It can also force you to see things you would not have been looking for without the failure. There are consequences to any failure, some very painful to be sure, but the recovery may end up leading you down a different path, so be open to what that opportunity may bring. Look for the open window when a door is shut.

ANALYZE THE FAILURE

Beware of confusing failure due to a poor decision with failure due to a character flaw like unethical behavior. I have seldom seen where you can fix a character flaw, but you can fix a mistake born of best intentions that simply resulted in a poor decision. When you do have the best intentions and fail, look for the root causes of the failure and correct those.

Tweaking what you have may not be the best approach. You may need to completely change your course of action if the root causes cannot be changed. Be willing to throw out the previous idea or action and start with a clean slate to get to your desired end state without the baggage you may have been inadvertently lugging around that led to the previous misstep. As they say, the definition of insanity is doing the same thing over and over again and expecting a different result. So, when you do fail, don't repeat insanity.

TRUST

As a leader, you cannot micromanage your way to success. The higher up you get in an organization, the more you need to let go of control and empower people to take calculated risk and push the envelope and—yes—fail. This can make some leaders uncomfortable, because they remain accountable for the results. But if you establish and maintain trust with your subordinates, make sure they understand the boundaries in which they can freely operate, and know the risk tolerance within the larger organization, you can provide them the framework to act decisively and boldly.

Your team members are normally the experts in their particular areas, and the more you give them free rein to be creative and collaborative across the organization, the more they will surprise you with ideas that you would not have thought of yourself. When they own the idea, they own the outcome. Reward creative and thoughtful collaborators publicly. It is particularly important to reward success after a failure and to emphasize that failure is not a career killer.

BE A LEADER

Again, be comfortable working and leading where things are not black and white but are nuanced or ambiguous. Being able to do so with confidence is why someone decided to put you in your leadership position, so own it. Be realistic and self-aware about your own weaknesses. Surround yourself with talented people who have strengths in areas you don't, then trust and empower them. Allow people to respectfully challenge your position on a topic, and thoughtfully listen to those contrary positions. It will be your decision in the end, and you are accountable to own the success or failure of that decision. If you have considered second- and third-order effects, any repercussions, and possible outcomes— good or bad—you will have greater confidence in your decision to move forward.

Taking other viewpoints into consideration is not intended to take an inordinate amount of time or delay decision-making. You will be making imperfect decisions with imperfect or incomplete information frequently, but avoid admiring the problem, which leads to decision paralysis, indecisiveness, or death by committee. Understand the risks, make the decision, and move out.

The more senior you are in an organization, the more gravity increases, personally and professionally, from a failure and when taking risk. This is normally due to the impact of the risk taken and if that impact is significantly miscalculated. At senior levels, a failure will normally affect a lot of resources and people, including external stakeholders and customers, so its impact can be felt across the enterprise. It is often an unintended or unplanned consequence that results in some failure. Show how you handle the impact of the failure, learn from it, and move on to achieve success later. It is important to set the tone within an organization.

On a personal level, your hard-earned reputation can be what's at risk. You can overcome this fear by establishing a reputation over time for strong leadership, good judgment, transparency, integrity, and teamwork—particularly if you've had a failure in the past that you turned around into a later success. People will remember and be tolerant of a bump in the road.

You are not on the journey alone. You have peers, mentors, family, friends, subordinates, and others who are there to help. Reach out to them. They may often feel like they cannot help you much, but they can, even if it is just to lend an ear and listen as you work through a problem or difficult time. When your weaknesses are identified, show that you can change behavior when given constructive feedback. Ask for that feedback in both informal and formal ways and visibly tie changes to the feedback you received. Your ultimate success depends on that group all around you who help enable your success.

When you were a kid and learning to ride a bike, you felt excited, proud, free, and confident at what you were doing. All the while, someone was in front of you—your mom, your dad, some crazy uncle—clearing away obstacles so you didn't wipe out and holding the back of the bike steady until you were off on your own. When you fell, they helped you up and didn't take the bike away. They got you right back on and had you try again, talking about what you could do better to avoid the fall next time. Before you knew it, you were leaving them in your dust as you pedaled down the street with the wind in your hair and bugs in your teeth. The same concept applies in your career: Don't be afraid to get bugs in your teeth.

When you face failure, those around you will learn from how you handle yourself with grace, intelligence, and determination to do what's right. In the end, that is the lesson that will matter most.

SEA STORY

INSERT FOOT IN MOUTH; CHEW VIGOROUSLY

I was at a meeting in the Pentagon, one of a thousand soul-crushing meetings that should have been an email, briefing a room full of very senior admirals, other officers, and civilian stakeholders, along with many more people joining via video teleconference. The topic was related to Navy networks and the information technology infrastructure.

continued

As always, when briefing these types of highly technical issues to folks who are not familiar with the terminology or who feel overwhelmed in understanding it, the briefer has to be cognizant of the audience and keep the discussion engaging, using terms and concepts that everyone can relate to. In the information technology world, we tend to "dolphin speak," using high-pitched squeaky noises that only those of us in that nerd club understand. This alienates, confuses, or simply pisses off everyone else. Practitioners who are very good in this field find a way to translate those highly technical terms into English, using layperson's terms that everyone can grasp and rally around.

So, there I was at the front of the room, brief going swimmingly, everything on track, when my mouth moved faster than my brain. Now, for anyone who knows me, they know this was not an isolated incident. My mouth is normally my biggest foe, whether for something I said or something I ate (like a whole box of those evil Girl Scout Samoas cookies in one sitting—carb coma to follow). I am from New York, so add to that unfortunate trait that I also speak very fast. In the middle of the brief, I was talking about our information technology architecture and what we were improving.

As I got to the portion where we were discussing that in more detail, I was supposed to say "the systems and technical architecture."

Instead, what I said was "the testicle architecture."

Cue awkward silence and uncomfortable glances around the room. You know those slow-moving videos where the train is derailing and there is some hapless guy standing right next to the tracks picking flowers, his feet seemingly planted in cement, and you know his head is about to get popped off like a bottle rocket? That is what it felt like at the podium. I had a split second to think of what to say, because it couldn't be unsaid at that point. It was the turd in the punchbowl, the fart in church.

So, I put my finger up and said, "What the admiral meant to say," and everyone started to laugh. "Now that I have your attention, and everyone in video teleconference-land is awake again, let's get back to the network."

I guess it met the criteria for keeping the conversation engaging and using language commonly understood. A little humor quickly diffused a professionally awkward situation.

Now I could have replayed that cringe-worthy scenario in my head like a bad movie for days afterward, but I chose not to. It was water under the bridge, couldn't be changed, and was not worthy of further beating myself up about it. Most people in the room (except my dear friends who, to this day, bring it up like it was their favorite blooper reel—"Hey, remember that time you said . . .") have long since forgotten about it. It was a nothing burger to them. If no one will remember or care three years from now, don't worry about it or waste your time and energy on it. Embrace your "testicle moment" and move on.

THREE POSITIVES

1. Everyone paid attention to the brief after the gaffe, so I made sure to get the key points in right after we started back up.

2. For once, the video teleconference was reliable and stayed up, normally a communications officer's dream but not in this situation—well done, IT support staff!

3. Never take yourself too seriously. Forgive yourself the gaffe and enjoy the humble pie.

TWELVE

OVERCOMING YOUR OWN BIASES

Mentoring is a multidimensional activity. It is important to be aware of factors that influence the mentor-mentee relationship. We all have biases and preconceived notions about the ways of the world. These notions are based on how we were raised, our values, religion, lifestyle preferences, careers, families, external cultural influences, and so on. Some of these biases are hardwired in childhood and difficult to recognize in ourselves or to be objective about. We need to be reflective and aware of our potential biases, keeping them in check so we do not project them onto those we mentor and unintentionally cloud good advice.

Let's take a few minutes to look at how our biases can affect our thinking and leadership decisions if we are not savvy enough to be aware of them. While you can sometimes make some broad characterizations about others, that can be, as we say in the Navy, "shoal waters," meaning it's a dangerous place to sail. Be cautious of projecting biases on an individual that simply don't apply.

Generational stereotypes can be particularly unhelpful. I often hear people say, "Millennials are entitled and lazy and expect to be rewarded for just doing their job. They need a lot of direction and hand-holding and are not loyal to employers. They expect others to snowplow problems out of their way." Interestingly, as with most stereotypes, the data do not support those presuppositions. One could make the same case for anyone, regardless of age, frankly. I know fifty-year-olds who act that way.

Be wary too of industry-specific stereotypes, but be mindful that industries do have certain cultures that drive behavior, results, perceptions of excellence, potential, and success. For example, sales executives and entrepreneurs did not get to where they are by being overly risk-averse introverts who take a long time to deliberate on decisions. On the other hand, engineers are more methodical and deliberate. I wouldn't want nuclear engineers shooting from the hip. "I'll take that 30 percent solution, partner!" Yikes! Steady, cowboy!

Gender and sexuality are also areas where many of us harbor unconscious biases. Seeing a mentee only as their gender, sexuality, or outward identity can have a disastrous effect on your ability to see the person behind these particular traits. Their skills, intellect, and integrity are not limited—or even affected—by these traits. Be aware of your own thoughts, and if you find yourself limiting your mentee to a particular category instead of assessing their true value, stop it. It won't help you, and it certainly won't help them.

By starting with a preconceived notion of how a mentee is likely to behave based on a stereotype, you limit their potential and fail to

provide the benefit of truly helping them to find greatness in themselves. You may not even realize it, but you may use language that
subtly but destructively supports those stereotypes or causes the person to perceive artificial barriers that don't actually exist.

INTERGENERATIONAL MENTORING

As I've already mentioned, take care to not fall prey to hidden generational biases. The people you mentor will come from backgrounds
that can differ widely from your own, and they may already have
a set of experiences that have shaped their decision-making and
thinking in different directions. By really getting to know them, you
will be able to understand those perspectives better and will be able
to understand why they perceive the world a certain way. You also
will better understand their values and decision calculus and will be
able to help broaden their thinking in new ways or reinforce the best
of what they already do.

Much has been written in recent years about the differences
between age groups, and many stereotypes have emerged that are,
frankly, unhelpful. Those generalizations don't apply in most cases,
and we should go in with eyes and ears open to find the true essence
of the person we are mentoring. Each person is an individual,
unique unto themselves, not to be conveniently binned so we know
how to "handle" them.

Don't make assumptions about anything when mentoring.
Engage in dialogue and find out. Ask, listen, discuss, and be open
with your mentees so they will feel comfortable to reciprocate that
openness with you. Find out what their value system is, what motivates them, what discourages them, and what they see as their own

strengths and weaknesses. Ask how they define success, how they like to communicate (both in the manner in which they express themselves through their words, body language, and actions and in their means of communications), and how they express emotions, empathy, courage, fear, acceptance, and disapproval.

At the end of the day, most people I have mentored have similar values and want the same things. Salary and compensation take a backseat to having their ideas thoughtfully considered, to their work being challenging and valuable to them, and to its being valued by their leadership. They want to do well at their work and be recognized for it—not in a public Best Cup of Coffee Ever Award but in how they are respected and treated by their leadership and the team they work with, in fair compensation, and in opportunities to advance. They want to be able to provide a decent life for their families and themselves, and they want to feel like the work they are doing is appreciated, important, and makes a difference.

I have found that my younger mentees and workers like more frequent and detailed feedback. Instead of saying, "Good job on the network project," I might say, "I really liked how you resolved that sticky situation with the network upgrade project and got the contractor to take a different approach, which let everyone stay online and continue working without interruptions. That was really resourceful work. Well done." The second way of providing feedback sends a clear message that you really understand what they did and that you recognize their level of effort and ingenuity. By the same token, set clear expectations of your mentees, and if they are not meeting those expectations, tell them quickly and unambiguously. Ask them to think through how they can improve before you provide your recommendations.

When mentoring people much younger than me, which is just about everyone at this point, discussing situations I have faced and asking how they would resolve or improve the situation teaches them *how* to think about problems, not *what* to think. After they talk about how they would handle it, we talk through possible outcomes of that approach, other factors that could come into play, and unexpected consequences that could result and how the mentee would deal with them. Then I tell them how I handled the situation. If I told them what I had done in that situation first, I would limit their ability to work through an issue and learn how to think about a problem or challenge themselves.

There can be differences in how people of different generations communicate. This really revolves around differences between digital natives and the rest of the crowd. Young people tend to be more at ease with adapting to and trusting emerging technology for communications than those who did not grow up in the internet age, but there are always exceptions. The important thing is to find out what medium the mentee prefers for communications and meet them there. They may discount the importance of the face-to-face meeting, but that has value as well if you can do it. The virtual face-to-face on a video teleconference or web meetup is also a good alternative, particularly if the discussion will be of a sensitive nature or if it is important to have the discussion in real time and to see their body language and facial expressions. Words do not always completely or accurately convey our messages clearly. Seeing the whole picture is important so meaning and emphasis are not lost or misinterpreted.

I have also seen changes in the formality of communication over the years. Today, younger people seem less formal in their speech and writing, particularly when they are used to the short-burst style of texting or Twitter. Sometimes that style bleeds over into the work-place, and the informality can come off as unprofessional or can inadvertently make it difficult for them to be taken seriously. They may also see less importance in a communications hierarchy and can be perceived as disrespectful to someone higher in the organization; they may think they are simply engaging on a personal level but are seen as amateurish. The tone for this is set in the organization, and for them to be effective, they will need to understand that. Discuss this with your mentees to help them gauge their organization's tone and expectations. It will raise their awareness of the effectiveness of their written and oral communications style.

The timing and frequency of communication are important as well, and I have found that the younger people I mentor are less interested in structured times, like monthly or quarterly scheduled meetups. They prefer instead to address issues episodically as they come up. This may be a bit more difficult to manage, given your own busy schedule, but you should accommodate it when possible. You could consider it just-in-time mentoring, but I prefer to think of it as a running unforced conversation. Just be clear about your expectations about how much advance notice you would need to accommodate meetups in this more ad hoc style of inter-action. Also, many younger folks work in the gig economy, so their schedules are varied and unpredictable. Having some flexible and agreed-on ground rules on communication will ensure that neither of you is frustrated.

An important part of mentoring young people is to be able to show your vulnerability as a leader and to share that your road to suc-cess had bumps along the way that may have sidelined you but did not stop you. Think back to what it felt like to be a twenty-two-year-old in your first job. Possibly throw in life issues like a first apartment, a first love, a first child, your first time managing finances, the first time you tied your own shoes, or the first time you vacationed in Middle Earth. Not everyone matures and grows at the same pace.

The world is a different place from when you grew up. Social media adds pressure to young people to feel like they have to be 100 percent successful all the time or they are a complete failure. Let's face it, Instagram influencers don't normally become successful by showing what an epic failure they are, with their tongue stuck in the keyboard. It's all about success, being at the top of the game and in lush locations, and being a free-spirited adventurer or a highly successful entrepreneur. That is the sizzle reel world most under twenty-five grew up in. When they see someone being successful, they are seeing the end state, not the struggle it took to get there. They need you to help them understand that success did not happen in an internet minute; it likely took years of hard work; planning; support from teammates, family, and friends; bumps along the way; and changes in course and speed. When they look at you as their mentor, they will see success, but again that success was years in the making. So, discuss your vulnerabilities and shortcomings and how you managed them on your journey.

GENDER BIAS

Gender is another example of a hidden bias. Young girls are bombarded with images of what women do and wear, how they should behave, and what careers they are encouraged to pursue. In recent years, awareness has improved, but we still have a long way to go until the day when no one in the workforce notices whether you identify as male, female, or nonbinary and where everyone is truly considered equal. The #MeToo movement also spurred greater awareness across society, not just in traditionally male-dominated professions.

In my Navy experience, I always wanted to be seen only as an officer, not as a female officer, and I managed my words and actions to support that. However, I also understood that it was important for more junior women to see other women advance in rank to senior levels. It mattered to show that there is no glass ceiling and that success is determined irrespective of gender, based on performance and potential. I had excellent female role models that showed me this, and I never felt gender to be a limiting factor.

Plus, growing up with three brothers prepared me very well for the male-dominated Navy. In our house, someone was always getting shanked, shot in the head with a BB gun, or falling victim to some other shenanigans, so you had to hold your own both physically and in the battle of wits. I even remember having it out with my grandmother when I was ten and she was babysitting for a weekend while my folks were off in a tennis tournament. After dinner, she excused the boys (precious cherubs) to go out and play and said that the girls (she and I, aka her lowly indentured servant) could do the dishes. I let her know in no uncertain terms that we all had jobs around here, and that included the boys, who were equally capable of washing dishes. If they weren't doing their jobs, I said, then I was not doing mine either. The result? Dishpan hands for the boys that day. Thanks, Gram, for understanding.

I was also fortunate to have a mother who never viewed things in terms of gender. It just never came up, and she never used it as a reason something could not be accomplished. In her mind, anything was and is possible with smarts, tenacity, heart, and soul; gender wasn't even a factor. She let me and my brothers know we could do or be anything, as long as we worked for it and didn't give up. She was an occupational health nurse, as well as a full-time mom, and great at both. At seventy-six, she still plays a 4.0 tennis game, can do anything, and was up on my roof the other day fixing a leak. If you need PVC pipe laid in your front yard or an antique Victrola repaired, she is your gal (and now, with YouTube videos, she is particularly dangerous). She does this without distraction of external judgment or perceived barriers—particularly, gender barriers—and taught me to do the same. Having role models like that when you are young matters.

That is not to say there was not discrimination, subtle or not, in the Navy. When I first joined, in 1989, it was everywhere. In fact, women weren't even allowed to serve on combat ships. But when I left, in 2019, I am happy to say that I didn't see overt discrimination and hadn't seen it firsthand for several years.

Gender distinctions became less overt over time and shifted from outright discrimination to subtle biases instead. These biases are still a part of most of us, and it will help your mentees if you are aware of your own and are able to smash them like my mom's ace serve. Biases appear now as offhand comments or unintentional terms or phrases that separate groups. For example, when starting meetings, they used to begin with "Gentlemen," regardless of who was in the room. My first few years in the Navy, I would blow it off and not say anything. The juice wasn't worth the squeeze. But as I rose through the ranks, I came to realize that I needed to correct it—not because it was important to me personally but because it mattered to get it right for the women junior to me. So, I would immediately add "and ladies" with a pleasant smile, and the speaker would course-correct. The best way to deal with those situations is to address them head-on in a polite way. In most cases, the person making the comment is not doing so intentionally or has not made themselves clear.

Thirty years ago, when I started in the Navy, I did not think in terms of gender, but it quickly became apparent that others did. They had biases that I became aware of and had to manage. Some sailors had never worked for a woman before. Many had no issues and adapted quickly, but some needed more instruction or were just resistant to change, period. Leadership, confidence, and excellence in your job win the day in the end, regardless of gender, so that is where I focused my efforts. Those who were openly hostile to women and remained in the "no opposable thumbs" category eventually retired or were weeded out. Today's Navy is a place I would be proud to have my daughter, sister, mom, or friend join and where I know they'll be treated equally with great respect, where opportunity is endless and knows no rank glass ceiling.

Understand how hidden biases can lead to additional scrutiny of your actions. For example, if you are a woman or minority in a position of power, there could be extra scrutiny of your words and actions. Have your antenna up and be aware that everything you say or do will be under a microscope and discussed after the fact. It may be something you say or do that is offhand or something you consider insignificant, but it may not be to someone else. If your words or actions are misinterpreted through some hidden bias, quickly clear it up through precise communication about what you intended the action or message to be. Be aware and stand by what you say and do.

SOCIETAL INFLUENCES
ON GENDER ROLES

In recent years, with the emphasis on nontraditional roles for women, role models abound. Women have achieved exceptional accomplishments across all industries from finance and commerce to the military, medicine, academia, politics, and science. That being said, we still have a ways to go to make it so that gender isn't even an issue discussed in the future, where being smart is more valued than being pretty, and "ambitious" and "assertive" are deemed equally positive qualities when talking about men or women.

Images of what girls can be when they grow up get shaped at a very young age. These images and societal norms influence thinking for both girls and boys, and later, for women and men, that carries over into the workplace. Just like my image of what a person could achieve was shaped by women like my mom and other strong women I was lucky enough to know, other societal factors can help shape those ideals for both men and women about gender roles, particularly when it comes to leadership and positions of authority.

Think about the toys that young girls play with, and while I will call out a few examples here, these are just a few of the hundreds I could have chosen from. Lego makes toy sets for girls, and top sellers include the summer pool, treehouse, pizzeria, art stand, café, friendship house, enchanted castle, friendship cakes, and so on. The Women of NASA set is an option but not as popular. For boys the top sellers are the NASA Apollo Saturn rocket, classic block-building set, police station, pirate roller coaster, construction site, Jurassic World, Ideas Ship in a Bottle, and the Hogwarts Express. Think how differently those are marketed to sell to each of those groups. I suspect that both groups could use a broadening of perspective about gender and toys that could resonate across both genders.

The goal would be to open up a more wide-ranging perspective for gender-neutral toy marketing and increased awareness of the messages being subtly sent to both boys and girls in their formative years.

In the past few years, Mattel, which makes Barbie dolls, has gone to great lengths to show Barbie in a different light, more progressive and career-focused. Until fairly recently, Barbie's top jobs were Mermaid and Princess, great work if you can get it (if only I could have landed one of those jobs instead of naval officer, but alas I lacked qualifications like couth, an hourglass figure, and fins). There were the occasional nods over the years to careers (president, computer scientist, astronaut), but did you ever see those in the advertising around Christmastime or were they the "also ran" categories? Remember, second place is the first loser. In fact, I remember doing a search a couple of years back for career Barbies on the Mattel website, and it took me to about page five to get beyond the glamour gals to someone with a real job: "Pizza Chef." Then it took me to the last page to get to a scientist. How I knew she was a smart scientist was she was wearing hideous glasses and holding a beaker. In all fairness, poor Ken didn't fare much better. His top jobs were Fashionista and Groom, and you normally found old Ken in the accessories aisle next to shoes and handbags. I mean really, wasn't he just a freeloader with a groovy camper hanging out at Barbie's dream house, eating all her food and working on his surfing skills?

Today, thankfully, Barbies come with more options that can spread a positive message for girls to consider careers like judge, entomologist, and marine biologist, and those images need to be pushed as hard or harder than the mermaids, princesses, and fashionistas. Heck, it doesn't have to be exclusive; Supreme Court Barbie can wear whatever she wants, including a mermaid tail.

In the South, they have a great expression that goes like this: "Bless their heart . . ." Now this normally comes with some side head shake and a sweet smile and is meant to say, "They are trying . . . but remain jacked up." In Barbie's case, I think total success will be achieved when Barbie's standard foot can accommodate a pair of Chuck Taylors (my footwear of choice) instead of being permanently molded for five-inch stilettos and her thighs actually touch. The size of her chest alone defies gravity and would make it almost impossible not to tip over if she were an actual person, especially in those stilettos. I know they developed a curvy Barbie a few years back and reduced the distance between her thighs, from something like you could drive a beer truck between to maybe a scooter—who knows, they may actually touch when pressure is applied. While there are women out there whose thighs don't touch, I think they are scarce—right up there with unicorns, Bigfoot, and rational presidential candidates. The Barbie "Inspiring Women" collection included such greats as Rosa Parks, Katherine Johnson, and Frida Kahlo. But again, "bless their hearts . . ." They still look like Marilyn Monroe playing those parts, but at least it's a step in the right direction. Rome wasn't built in a day, and neither will Barbie's thighs and waist. Honestly, I can't wait for the day when a Ms. Potato Head comes with an artificial intelligence chip that I can insert in her head instead of earrings, and she carries a computing device instead of a purse. Think of the message that would send to young girls.

MIND YOUR OWN BIASES

We all have environmental and societal ideals pushed on us from all angles, and it can be easy to have hidden biases cloud our better judgment or hamper our decision-making as leaders. Put your self-awareness antenna up and keep it there to avoid being on the wrong side of the discussion. You have a responsibility to discover and understand and to eliminate or manage your biases. It's not enough just to acknowledge them. For example, make an effort to steer clear of focusing on the physical and being too quick to judge on a first impression. It is human nature to try to "bin" people into categories as you meet them, to try to predict or understand how they will act. We all do it. Resist making those assumptions. Our unconscious bias can seep in, and we may not see or appreciate the person's full potential, which is unhelpful for the whole team. Don't be fooled by contrived "packaging" or slick talk. Be astute enough to look beyond the superficial and see the substantive.

What interests me is what is in someone's head and in their heart, not how they look, and I never put form over function. Remember, the shell doesn't define us; the spirit does. That takes more effort to discern, and you find that out through honest interpersonal inter-action. Have a conversation and get to know your mentee, your team members—anyone. Ask questions. Let them do the talking while you listen. Ultimately, their actions and performance are the true indicators of their character, worth, and potential, and you will learn it over time. Just don't be distracted by physical appearance at your first meeting and pigeonhole the person in a way that may limit their potential contributions to the team and organization. Discover the substantive, and you will find your superstars.

As a mentor, you should understand the context of your men-tee's thinking and value system and, most important, you should get to know them as a person by asking thought-provoking questions that get to the essence of who they are and what shapes their think-ing and lives. This means that you need to do more listening than talking. How often have you been in a conversation where you can tell that the other person is just working through in their mind what they think you are going to say next and formulating their response as opposed to intently listening? Did they hear not just what you said, the actual words you used, but also the message you meant to communicate? Listening also involves what you are also *not* saying, the message your body language provides and the tone in your voice. All of those nuances of communication are important for a mentor to observe and act on.

Understanding how to pick up those subtle messages in a world with vastly different forms of communication—in person, web conferencing, chat, voice, and so on—can be a challenge, particularly where the preferred form of communication for your mentee is one you are not as comfortable with. For example, I don't mind chatting via text or instant messages with mentees on more superficial mentoring topics but still find communicating in person or face-to-face via the web more effective for the thornier issues so I can see my mentees and discern subtle voice inflections or body language that is hidden in chats, email, or other more stagnant media.

You will quickly distinguish between the performers and the posers. I've worked in high tech for years, and wearing a hoodie and the latest earbuds doesn't make you more creative, innovative, or out of the box than someone in a sweater vest and loafers, a uniform, or even overalls, a tinfoil hat, and a blow-up rubber ducky ring. Much like the misplaced self-righteousness of vegans and CrossFitters, it's just irritating—like sandpaper on your rear end.

RUN LIKE THE WIND BULLSEYE...

Can you imagine being stuck in an elevator with that trifecta of the techie in a hoodie, the vegan, and the CrossFitter? Yikes. That would be like having your head squeezed in an organic juicer with one hand by the CrossFitter with overdeveloped abs who's holding a ginormous truck tire in the other hand. I get that people think by dressing a certain way they are promoting an image or perception of themselves. But that is at best temporary and at worst completely superficial, so don't be fooled by it. Precious precociousness and self-promotion by focusing on form over function is a red herring, merely a distraction that experienced leaders are quick to see through. I find in one-on-one mentoring that the core values people find most important are consistent, regardless of age group or other demographics. People want to do well at work, have their work make a difference, and be acknowledged for their contributions.

You can overcome your biases by making a conscious effort to recognize them in yourself and by making sure that they don't taint your decision-making or get in the way of your relationship objectives. Take the time to get to know those you mentor and learn what motivates them. Seek common ground on shared values, objectives, goals, and interests. That, coupled with transparency and trust, is the foundation of a good mentor-mentee relationship.

SEA STORY

RACKING UP THE COMPLIMENTS

About ten years ago, I was in an organization called a "joint command," meaning it was made up of service members from the Army, Navy, Air Force, and Marine Corps. I was a commander at the time, a fairly senior officer, and most of the other people in the organization were of the same rank or one rank beneath that. There were about fifteen of us, and we sat in cubicles in a U-shaped space where we could just turn around to collaborate around a large table. It was a great group of professionals, all really good shipmates.

One day, I was wearing my white dress uniform instead of camouflage, our normal uniform of the day, because I

continued

was going to an event later that afternoon. The dress uniform had pins and other insignia on it that we don't wear with the camouflage uniform. One part of the uniform is a set of ribbons that represent the medals you have received for superior performance or participation in various military operations, worn above the left breast pocket. You can tell a lot about a person's military career just by reading their rack of ribbons and insignia.

That day, I walked into the bullpen of cubicles to talk to one of the other officers, and a Marine major, an enormously talented officer and leader who I admired a lot, a very by-the-book, straitlaced guy, turned to me and said loudly and enthusiastically, "Nice rack, ma'am!"

All the other officers in the bullpen spun their heads around like Linda Blair in *The Exorcist* sans vomit, with shocked expressions on their faces. I paused for a split second and saw the look of pure mortification on the major's face as we all mutually acknowledged it sounded like he was talking about my chest and not my ribbons.

He stammered, "Ah, ma'am, that didn't come out as I intended. What I meant to say was about your ribbons."

I quickly diffused everyone's discomfort with "Well, that's the nicest compliment I've gotten all day. I'm going to have to come over here more often. I can't wait to tell my husband."

He and everyone else started laughing. They teased him about it that day and for months afterward.

The context matters. This was an innocent mistake by a great guy that didn't need to be blown out of proportion.

If it had been a genuine show of the officer's bias, however, it would have warranted a discussion. I would have pulled him aside—no need to embarrass him in front of a group—and explained why the comment made me uncomfortable. Most likely, he'd understand, be mortified, and apologize; then we would move on with our lives, and he would learn something from it.

THREE POSITIVES

1. I was reminded not to be overly sensitive and to take comments in context, to recognize the innocent mistake.

2. Words can be heard and interpreted many ways by the listener, but words can fail us, so listen for intent in the words; this is particularly important in your mentoring and leadership roles.

3. Any compliment is a good one; thanks for brightening my day, Major.

THIRTEEN

GUARD YOUR REPUTATION AS A LEADER

A s you advance and grow in your career, you will establish your reputation. The choices you make in each job form an aggregate that will both precede and follow you. Be aware of how your actions are perceived by others so that you are comfortable with the reputation you establish. Others' opinions are formed by observing the way you lead and manage; how you align your words to your actions; how you treat subordinates, peers, and superiors; and how you make decisions, take risks, and innovate. You will need to demonstrate tenacity, humility, consistency, accountability, responsibility, authority, respect for others, commitment to the mission, poise under pressure, intellect, and wisdom—easy enough, right? Understanding how others see you enables you to better collaborate with them and to ensure you are meeting the high standards they expect.

Guard your reputation closely by being attentive and consistent in your actions and words. Understand that in more senior or high-visibility positions, everything you do will be scrutinized. Others will assume what your motives and intentions are. Honesty in your words and deeds helps to mitigate misinterpretation. Other factors may come into play as well that result in additional scrutiny, perhaps because you are a minority, a woman, or have been very successful elsewhere, so you have to be aware that you could be under even more of a microscope.

YOUR SOCIAL MEDIA NARRATIVE

Pay close attention to your narrative on social media and the internet. Once it is out there in the digital world, it is there forever—no taking it back. So, think before you post, tweet, blog, or comment. Double-check your distribution lists and who you connect with.

The internet is an amazing platform to get information out quickly and to audiences you would have never reached otherwise, to share ideas and collaborate. But be aware that others can use it for their advantage or to discredit you if they have an ax to grind. Deep fakes (where someone can manipulate video or voice images to make it seem like you have said or done something you have not) are easy to create and widely distributed now. They are even used by nation-states and other cyber hackers in disinformation campaigns. The more visible you are to the public in your role and the more senior you are in an organization, the more likely you could become victim to this type of social media attack. You can go back after false information is out to claim the inauthenticity of the material, but normally, the first story out is the one that sticks. After that horse has left the barn, it's hard to get it back in. If you are consistent and truthful with your thoughts and messages, people will be less likely to believe something posted that is outrageous or out of character for you.

Make sure the social media narrative you can control is the narrative you *do* control. Be savvy about where you are messaging and who the audience is. Choosing the best platform matters: LinkedIn is not the place to share videos of your taco pull-apart bread or the Vegas weekend with your friends (probably best left off of social media entirely), and Facebook is where Grandma hangs out, not where you will most likely reach Gen Z and Millennials. Texting and apps still rule the day for them; they would rather go without showers, food, cars, and a kidney than be without their phone with access to those apps.

Staying connected professionally via social media is very important today and can provide opportunities to spread your ideas, collaborate with a broader group, get good ideas from others, see opportunities for those you mentor, network with other professionals in your field, volunteer your time and talents to help others, and share "success kid" memes, videos of cats opening beer cans, and kids taking Sharpies to embellish the faces of younger siblings in diapers. The possibilities are basically endless, but use social media wisely. Many people look to "build their brand" or platform on social media. That sounds a bit too Hollywood for me, but be deliberate about what you put out on the internet and about the messages that can be implied or assumed by what you share. If you post something regrettable—we are all human—own it and correct it quickly. Don't let an undisciplined internet presence in your personal life affect your professional life and reputation.

As you mentor people, be sure to ask them about their internet presence and digital lives. But first, do a bit of snooping on them yourself so you can provide some examples of the good and the not-so-good (e.g., the award for 2018 Beer Pong Champion of the Eye Tappa Keg fraternity is unlikely to earn your mentee a promotion). Give them guidance on how to make good choices and to craft their own story.

AVOIDING POTHOLES ON THE LEADERSHIP HIGHWAY

Leadership is in part innate. Your vision, empathy, and ability to work hard, for example, are skills that are hard to learn and more usually just a facet of who you are. The other part of leadership is learned through experience. You need to have different skills for each kind of leadership, and you will learn what you need as you move to positions of greater power, authority, and influence. Struggling as you learn those skills is normal, and we all make mistakes.

If you make a misstep, you will likely be under additional scrutiny to see whether your mistake was an isolated incident or a performance deficiency. You will have to expect and respond appropriately, not defensively, to that additional scrutiny. Don't let your misstep affect the great leadership traits you have, but do let it be an opportunity for transparency in your leadership. For example, if the incident was based on a formal complaint against you about unfair treatment or discrimination, your subsequent words and—more important—your actions should show how you want to ensure that you lead an organization in which you do not tolerate discriminatory behavior and in which people do not feel intimidated or unable to speak up.

Reality doesn't always win. Whether the original complaint against you was true or not is irrelevant. The perception is there for those who complained, and possibly for others. Perception can end up becoming reality, so be attuned to how it can impact your effectiveness, particularly the more senior or powerful the position you hold. As with social media, the first story told is the one that usually sticks, so it's important to try to control that messaging whenever you can to ensure that the facts are known.

If you did make a mistake, admit it and communicate that message clearly. While that's not always easy, it should not make you afraid to do what you need to do or say what you need to say. Continue to have the courage and heart to take the right actions, regardless of personal consequences—but be aware of the implications of how people may perceive your words and actions. The more important and visible you are in your organization, the more this will be your reality.

Provide context

It's important to distinguish what your position means in terms of your personal leadership. The more senior or powerful you are in an organization, the more you will have real or perceived power to influence the lives and decisions of others. With power comes increased scrutiny. The higher you are up the food chain, the more your every action is judged, often without context or by the uninformed, who do not know your true intentions if you have not communicated them well.

If you know what you are going to say or do could be misinterpreted, provide context. You never need to justify to subordinates why you are doing something or your decision, but you can provide context, which helps them understand how they can have a supporting role. Make sure they understand why their part is important. Make your communication consistent, transparent, and frank, and be willing to hear and act on constructive criticism.

Curate your culture

While 90 percent of the people you work with will be respectful and supportive, just as you are to them as their leader, others will be jealous, manipulative, sycophantic, or at worst, deceptive. You have to realize that there are people like that out there and that those are character flaws you cannot change. You can only root them out like a cancer by making sure the message is clear to everyone around you that those behaviors don't meet your high standards and aren't tolerated. When you find those negative influences, get rid of them quickly. Do it by the book and document everything.

Know and manage relationships with those that have influence in the organization—good or bad. They may be in a position of power or just be someone that everyone trusts or goes to. If they are a good, supportive influence, use them to help with your messaging and to advance your efforts. If they are a bad influence, give them one warning, then get rid of them. You do not have to suffer fools, and those types of employees need to be called out on their bad behavior. It can be destructive on many levels, including to personal relationships or relationships with those external to the organization, and in not supporting progress to implement new ideas or not encouraging challenges to the status quo.

Action against the negative influence needs to be taken swiftly and decisively. When giving the person the chance to correct their toxic behavior, leave no room for interpretation of your expectations and how their improved performance or behavior will be measured and documented. If you do remove someone, be transparent to the rest of the organization that they did not meet the standards and have been removed. Don't just quietly sweep it under the carpet.

ADDRESSING COMPLAINTS

Anyone in a leadership position knows you can't make everyone happy all the time. Frankly, that's not your job, and you are not there to be their friend. Your job is to excel at your critical mission, to meet or exceed what you've been hired for. In the process of doing that, of course, you take care of people. That means not just paying lip service to the "people are my most important asset" lingo but doing the hard work of making sure you act on it. Your people should be treated fairly and honestly and should have a safe work environment where they feel like they are part of the team and that their contributions are valued.

To do that, you need to get back to the basics. Do they receive their performance appraisals on time? Do the appraisals actually reflect the work your employees do? Are your team members paid on time and correctly? Do you (or your subordinate managers in larger organizations) provide clear expectations and guidance? Is the workplace safe—free from both physical and nonphysical threats to their well-being? Do you articulate and enforce workplace values consistently and publicly? Do you make it clear that discrimination of any kind is not tolerated? You should follow up any allegations with swift, decisive investigations and action. Do you have development plans for each of your employees based on their personal and professional goals, and are you actively helping them to achieve those goals? Do you ensure that everyone has a good mentor? Do you provide space to think and allow time to step back, so your team can look at what they do and how things could be improved for the organization? Do you thoughtfully consider recommendations for changes or improvements? Do you elicit their input and feedback, particularly in areas where they are subject matter experts? Do you look for opportunities to publicly recognize outstanding performance through formal awards or comments at meetings or walkabouts? Do you deal with substandard performance or disciplinary issues promptly, legally, and with transparency? Do you ensure that your human resources department has issued clear policies and guidance and that those are enforced uniformly across the organization? Do you have mechanisms for feedback, formal and informal, and the means to do so anonymously? Do you communicate strategic vision and goals clearly to the team so they understand your priorities and how their efforts align?

Even if you do all of these things—and do them well—there is still a possibility that someone could be unhappy—even enough to lodge a formal complaint against you. These complaints can run the gamut from creating a hostile work environment or being a bully to making someone do something that they are unqualified or unpaid for or that is outside their assigned responsibilities. It can also involve not taking care of issues raised concerning other employees or managers in the organization. You often find out about those issues through formal complaints submitted to a human resources or legal department, via a survey gauging employee satisfaction, from others in the organization, or perhaps from an anonymous complaint on a hotline or in a suggestion box.

When you receive a complaint, you need to conduct a prompt and thorough investigation into the veracity of the alleged issue. If the issue concerns you, stay out of that investigation until it is done and do not try to influence it. Let an unbiased third party, most likely your human resources or legal department in a large organization, look into it and present a finding of facts, assumptions, and recommendations for action.

The allegation could be against you personally or against the organization. Regardless, it could be very hurtful for you to hear, particularly if you know it to be untrue or you were unaware that you were behaving in a way that was perceived differently by others. When something like that happens, take a moment for self-reflection and to question whether the way you act or speak could have caused the issue. Frequently, we are under pressure to get something done; sometimes that pressure is self-induced, and sometimes it is externally applied, but we may push that pressure onto our subordinates. If you truly know your team, you will be able to see the subtle signs of too much pressure and will be conscious of that. Keep it on your radar to look for those warning signs and shield your subordinates from unnecessary pressure.

SEA STORY

"YOU'RE NAKED!"

When my daughter was about fifteen years old, she had three of her friends sleeping over for the night. Now, I loved a good sleepover, because it normally consisted of the girls lounging around doing their thing on their cell phones—texting each other from the same sofa, posting every waking moment to Instagram or Twitter, taking 450 pictures of their big toes after adding face filters and setting that to music, and so on—but most of all, lots of giggling and raucous noise. It made the house come alive in a way that you have to stop and appreciate.

Well, this particular night, things had slowed down, and the girls had exhausted all their activities, like making some inedible science project in the kitchen. This is inevitably filled with tons of sugar and butter, and they surely eat most of it before it gets anywhere near the oven. No matter how bad it turns out, the remains are reserved for my husband because, of course, "Dad eats anything." Because they were looking for something to do, I suggested, "Hey, let's watch some home movies from when you were a baby. Those are always fun."

A teenager staple, the eye roll, from my daughter. But her friends egged her on, and before long, everyone was all in, especially when I recommended that critically acclaimed favorite, the naked baby video. What teenager doesn't want to show naked baby videos of themselves to their friends, am I right? So, good sport that my daughter is, she was up for a little teenage humiliation and agreed. In went the video, and we were off to the races.

The video starts off with us on one of those ginormous ships, taking a cruise through the Panama Canal. My daughter was eighteen months old at the time and cute as a button. We were in our cabin on the ship getting ready to go to the pool. As all kids love to do, she was running around, buck naked, as we tried to catch her to put her bathing suit on. There is something about kids and not wearing a stitch of clothes; something brings out the exhibitionist streaker in all of them. Thankfully, most of us grow out of this. There is this sense of freedom seldom replicated in adulthood when jiggling and dangly bits get in the way of that unabashed freedom of movement.

So, there she was, running all over as I videotaped her, yelling "naked baby!" to which she responded with joyous peals of laughter as she would run by us and we would fake trying to catch her, only to have her "escape" at the last second for more laps around the room. The girls were watching the video and laughing at how silly and cute she was when my daughter turned to me in complete horror and said, "Mom, you're *naked!*"

I looked at her, not understanding what she meant, and said, "No, honey, *you're* naked. You know, 'Naked baby! Naked baby.'"

continued

My daughter, face beet red, replied, "Mom, look in the mirror."

Sure enough, off to the side of my wild daughter was a mirror. Clearly visible in the reflection is me, completely naked, only my face hidden from view by the video camera. It goes on for an excruciating amount of time. I cannot believe we did not notice that before. The girls started laughing even more now. But that was not the worst part.

The worst is when I think about how many copies of our vacation video we happily gave to relatives and friends—probably upward of ten copies. I can only imagine their reactions. "Does she know what she sent us?" before they too, I'm sure, burst into laughter. No one ever said a word to us about it, but this does explain a great many mysteries that have been unanswered since that fateful day, like why my mother-in-law has given me underwear and nightgowns like clockwork for Christmas for the past fifteen years. She would have probably sent a weed whacker too if postage from South America hadn't been too high.

Important safety tips for future reference: Refrain from holding recording devices while naked. Mirrors are not your friends; they are evil, so know where they are at all times. (This is a helpful tip for murders and other crimes you may be considering as well.) Never give your kid more ammunition for blackmail. They are also inherently evil and will use it to their advantage.

THREE POSITIVES

1. Thankfully, this was the age before social media, so the outlook remains positive that I will not be the next naked admiral viral sensation.

2. I realized I looked pretty good back then. I think I could actually make out an ab muscle on closer analysis of the footage. This motivates me to get back in shape . . . someday, or to deep fake a six-pack in any future videos.

3. I have captured on video what matters: my sweet daughter running around free as a bird and her joyous peals of laughter; no amount of personal embarrassment trumps that.

+ + +

Older folks can rejoice in the regrettable things they did that never made it to the internet, and the younger generation needs to be mindful that their whole lives will be in the cloud forever. Any crazy weekend can have an impact on your personal and professional life. If you can't avoid doing something stupid (and who among us can?), make sure there are no cameras.

FOURTEEN

YOU ONLY LIVE ONCE

D on't shortchange your health—take it seriously. You only go around this rodeo once. By taking care of your health, you are sending an important message to those you lead and mentor that it matters. It also matters to those who depend on you, care about you, and want you to succeed. It sends the message that you care about yourself and your life outside the workplace as much as you do about the job. This opens the door for your employees and mentees to take care of themselves too.

Through your actions, encourage your team and mentees to take care of their physical, mental, and emotional health. Your words are important, but your actions are what speak volumes. If someone is struggling, find out what they need and help them get that assistance. Make sure they feel supported to take care of their well-ness and not pressured to miss medical appointments for meetings or other work activities.

Dealing with mental and emotional health is particularly tricky, but if you know those you lead and mentor, you will know when they are "off" or just not themselves and you can talk to them about that. Make it clear that, at all levels of leadership, it's important to reach out and say, "Hey, you don't seem like yourself today. Is every-thing alright? Is there something I can help you with?" Be mindful and open to hearing feedback that you may be the cause of their stress. Not everyone can assume the same level of productivity or work effectively under the same stressful conditions, so be particu-larly attuned to body language and tone. The signs are subtle, and you could miss them. Having your antenna up to catch easily missed signs is important. A sideways glance, a sigh, a quick look of defeat, a change in tone, and a rote response are all slight gestures that can be missed but are indicative of a bigger problem.

Often, problems at work have a twin at home or with health-related issues. These problems can compound and, for some, can feel overwhelming, with no relief in sight. We put unre-alistic pressure on ourselves to do it all and to do it all well. Some will not ask for help or won't say they don't know something or that a task is too much for them. There can be an artificial fear of being seen as incapable, as not a team player, as going against organiza-tional culture, or as afraid of a challenge. However, the pressure on our psyche can become overwhelming and can manifest itself in behavioral and physical effects, particularly if coupled with other relationship, health, financial, or family concerns. Create a culture where it is OK to speak up and ask for help without adverse conse-quences. You must set the tone that you expect people to take care of themselves and to have actual work-life balance. (See Chapter 7 for more on work-life balance.)

If you have built up trust with your team and they know that you do have genuine concern for their well-being, they are more likely to ask for and get the help they may need. That includes taking care of health issues or their families. In some organizations, the employees may feel that seeking help for mental or emotional issues will put them at risk of losing their job or a promotion opportunity or that the personal information they share will be shared with others. A breach in trust may never be repaired, so be mindful and cautious that when a person is discussing issues of a highly personal nature, it took courage to even approach anyone about it. Reaching out to someone to show that you noticed something was not right could be the difference between their seeking help and feeling despondent. Those conversations are best done in person and in a private setting. Email, video teleconferencing, text, and other media are OK, but frank and difficult conversations are best conducted in person so the nuances in body language, voice tone and inflection, and words are not misinterpreted.

In the end, your health is your own. Balancing your own health—and allowing your team to balance theirs—with your work and all of your other interests involves conscious choices. The two most precious commodities you have are time and health, and neither is guaranteed, so never take them for granted. You owe it to those who love you to take care of your health.

You know when we get some new ache or pain and say, "Oh well. It's probably the burrito I ate," or "Oh well. I'm just getting old"? Don't "Oh well" your life away. Don't make excuses or let those who work with you do the same.

I can honestly say that if I died today, I would die without regrets. I've always been a carpe diem kind of gal, and I don't believe in bucket lists. Life is too short for that. Do that thing you've been putting off. And be a hypochondriac; it's OK to get that mole checked or to ask your doctor about that persistent ache. Most of all, be grateful for every day you have to make a difference before you make your exit.

SEA STORY

TOMORROW IS NOT PROMISED

In November 2018, I had a heart attack at only fifty-one years old. The crazy thing is that the week before, my husband and I had been hiking twelve miles a day in the mountains and rappelling and swimming around in caves in New Zealand. I had just gotten a clean bill of health from my doctor on my annual exam (albeit with the also annual cholesterol and "you need to lose weight" warnings). I had just taken my semiannual Navy physical fitness test and did well enough that I was exempt from portions of it the following spring. Then, walking around Annapolis Christmas shopping, I had a heart attack. It must have been sticker shock at the prices.

Anyway, the surreal part about the incident was that I didn't even know it was happening, which is often the case for heart attacks in women. Heart disease is actually the leading cause of death in women in the United States. According to the Centers for Disease Control and Prevention, heart disease kills about one in every four women, and about two-thirds of women who have heart attacks that lead to death had not experienced any symptoms.[2] That was me. So not

continued

2   "Women and Heart Disease," Centers for Disease Control and Prevention, https://www.cdc.gov/heartdisease/women.htm.

only was I a walking statistic (anything I can do to support the CDC), I was also a ticking time bomb.

As my husband and I were shopping, I just felt "off"—that is the best way to describe it. My chest felt a bit tight, like when you breathe in air deeply when you are outside running on a cold winter day and you have the sensation of a little burn in your chest.

I started doing what all of us do unless we are already predisposed to being a hypochondriac: I started making excuses. We all know the behavior I'm talking about. We "oh well" it away. Oh well, it's probably something I ate. Oh well, it's probably the extra push-ups I did on my physical fitness test yesterday. Oh well, I'm just getting old. Oh well, work is just stressing me out today. Oh well . . . HOW MUCH DOES THAT COST? Then, about thirty minutes later, I started to feel tired. So, again, I brought on the "oh wells." Oh well, I still have jet lag from our trip. Oh well, I have terrible sleep habits anyway. Oh well, we've been walking around all morning. Oh well, I'm just getting old, and did you see how much that cost!?

When I told my husband what I was feeling, he immediately said, "That's it; we're going to the emergency room." My husband was a physical therapy assistant who worked at inpatient facilities in hospitals for twenty years and is now a reiki master and volunteers giving treatments for wounded warriors and those with traumatic brain injuries. So not only is he a completely selfless guy, but he's seen it all medically and suffers no fools in that area. He's also a model of physical fitness and looks like he is about twenty-five years old. In fact, at a ceremony at work recently, he was standing with my daughter and me in a receiving line, and someone looked at the two of them and said to me, "Oh, are these your children?" First of all, he's Latino, so he looks nothing like me, and by the way, the guy is fifty-four. So, of course, I answered, "Well, actually, he's my husband, but I used to be his babysitter, so it's all good." It's sad when you go to a restaurant with your husband who is older than you and you are both carded—him to verify he is old enough to drink and me for the AARP discount. Anyway, I digress. Having worked in intensive care settings in hospitals for years, he knew my symptoms were something we needed to get checked out and pronto. I did what I suspect many of you would have done as well. I resisted.

"It's nothing!" I said. "Really, they are just going to give me Motrin and an eyeball roll for being a hypochondriac and send me home. I will be embarrassed if it's nothing. I've been trained to tough it out. I don't want to be a wimp. Really, this is nothing."

He was having none of that and replied that we were going, and if it turned out to be nothing, then fine. We go to the emergency room, and they eventually find out that the old widow-maker artery is 95 percent clogged. Off I go

continued

immediately to Stentville, followed up by the ever-popular twins of beta blocker medication and cardiac rehab. To say I was lucky is an understatement. To say I am blessed with a husband who cares enough to make me take warning signs seriously and get medical attention is also an understatement.

THREE POSITIVES

My three positives out of that incident are about being grateful.

1. First, I was grateful for my husband and his concern for me.
2. Second, I was grateful for the opportunity to have been given a warning shot on my health, a wake-up call that may have extended my life by years if I make the recommended lifestyle changes.
3. Third, I was grateful for the free bikini wax I got in prepping the artery in my upper thigh for surgery. Had I known I was going to get that, I would have considered the heart attack options years ago. Well played, surgery preop team, well played.

+ + +

A bonus positive is that I increased my focus on what matters. Time and health cannot be bought or bartered, and we are not promised tomorrow, so make a difference before you make your exit. Listen to your significant other, unless they have recently taken out a large life insurance policy on you and are encouraging you to take up skydiving or midlife cage fighting. In those cases, make them do it with you, so your story does not end up as a Lifetime movie or on a special edition of Investigation Discovery's *Who the (Bleep) Did I Marry?*

We all have people in our lives that we think the world of and they think the world of us. If you don't take care of your health for yourself, do it for them. Having a proper work-life balance and making sure you have taken care of their needs are important along your career journey. They will be there in your times of crisis. Look out for them as they look out for you by taking your health seriously. Listen to the warning signs your body gives you. If something feels "off," it probably is, and it is well worth getting checked out. If the worst thing to come out of it is that they send you home with Motrin and a slight ribbing about being the village hypochondriac, be grateful.

Maintaining your health is a commitment that takes sustained time and effort. While I don't feel any different from before the heart attack and have no visible, lasting effects, I know things are different and that I can make sure I am able to have the longest, healthiest life possible. I want to be around for my family and friends who, presumably, share that hope.

I also jokingly played the heart attack card at work after that to get things done faster, much to my boss's chagrin. In a meeting where a decision was languishing, I would dramatically clutch my chest, get a pained look on my face, and say, "Oooo! I am starting to get chest pains! Feeling a little short of breath here. Can we just not approve this now?" They would know I was joking, but it drove the point home: I can't wait forever for this decision, so make it. You've got to work with what you've got. Remember, never let a good crisis go to waste.

FIFTEEN

LEARN FROM THE JERKS

I have been lucky to work with some of the finest leaders in the nation—officers, chiefs, sailors, and government civilians. They are leaders of unquestionable character, integrity, and concern for those they serve. These people would have left success in their wake in any chosen career field, where they would have had more time with family and earned more money, but they chose to serve a higher calling: to defend the Constitution of the United States at great personal cost to themselves—in some cases, with their lives. I would have followed these people—representing all ranks, positions, and demographics—into battle without question. I learned from them, supported them 110 percent, felt inspired by them, and wished to emulate them. I took pieces of each of their leadership strengths and molded them into the amalgam of my own leadership style. Hopefully, I've also passed on their greatest attributes to those I have mentored along the way.

Most—maybe 95 percent—of the leaders I've worked with over the years fall into this category. I know I said I wasn't going to do public math, but this is an exception to my moratorium on the evils of mathematics because I can deal with this level of complexity. While 95 percent is impressive, it's not 100 percent. Who is that 5 percent? They are the jerks.

We all have our moments of less-than-stellar leadership under pressure, where we behave in a regrettable way. Hopefully those moments are few and uncharacteristic of our general leadership style. Unfortunately, for some leaders, those regrettable characteristics are the essence not just of their leadership style but of their personality. These people make a higher-level art form out of being a jerk.

We've all worked for jerks. You know the type of bosses I am talking about. Certain common traits live like a cancer in these people. They lack empathy and bully and humiliate their subordinates. They are calculating and manipulative in relationships, constantly attempting to influence others. They are unpredictable, take cheap shots, question loyalty and integrity, and try to make others feel guilty, unworthy, or inadequate. They seek personal advantages at the expense of others and see everyone else as competition. They are impatient, selfish, condescending, or sarcastic because they cannot express themselves in a constructive manner.

Unfortunately for the rest of us, jerks are often very smart and good at achieving results in their job, so they "manage up" well. Their bosses often think they are brilliant because they deliver, but they show a different face to the boss than they show to their peers and subordinates, making life miserable for everyone around them.

When the boss is finally informed of the problem, they are often incredulous. "How could it be possible? He is the top-performing division director and has achieved X, Y, and Z!" What the boss doesn't see—or, worse, turns a blind eye to as they are dazzled by the façade of success—is the jerk's sharp elbows and flaws. They don't see the demoralized subordinates and their team's lack of motivation to perform above minimum requirements.

Jerks are the kind of leader that goes around constantly reminding everyone they are in charge and relies heavily on positional authority as a crutch. Let me tell you: If you have to tell people you are the boss, then you carry that position in title only. Sadly, the problem with most jerks is that they also lack self-awareness of their behavior and its true impact. Or worse, they are complete narcissists who don't care. They are normally deeply insecure and feel like they have to behave that way to be "in control" or to be perceived as a "strong, confident leader." They become a comical or grotesque caricature of true leadership.

People are less loyal to organizations that support or are oblivious to toxic leadership. Even stellar employees will stagnate under a jerk's leadership. When they are forced to follow someone only because of positional authority, they will do only enough to get by, just enough to keep the jerk out of their face. In the worst circumstances, people become disenfranchised. This leads to an exodus of the best talent from the organization. People simply won't work for a jerk if they don't have to, and they will take their talents elsewhere. Organizations who don't root out the jerks end up awash in mediocrity and dysfunction. How much suffering and lost talent is one person's perceived success worth? I'd argue that your return on investment will be much better if you reform or remove the jerk from your organization.

CONFIDENCE—NOT ARROGANCE

Confidence in yourself is important and leads to others having confidence in you as well. However, there is a fine line between confidence and arrogance. People who are arrogant in many cases think they are projecting confidence and lack the self-awareness to understand how their behavior is being perceived. Those who mistake arrogance for confidence disrupt the work environment. A leader's arrogance and overblown ego are not only transparent to everyone around them, but they do not lead to success.

A key distinction between confidence and arrogance is that arrogant people make it seem like they have all the answers. This hubris leads to an erosion of trust, confidence, creativity, and productivity. The people beneath them in the organization will be reluctant to challenge them when they are wrong or to bring them recommendations or new ideas. They incorrectly assume "the boss already knows; she has the answers and will tell us what to do."

Leaders who act this way are full of self-doubt. They have let their insecurities creep in, and you can tell deep down that they probably question their ability to successfully operate at their level. In many cases, the skills that got them to their current position are not the same skills they need to be effective at the new level, so they overcompensate through arrogant or defensive behavior. They are extremely sensitive to criticism and negative feedback. They see criticism as a challenge to their authority. So, don't let your ego get in the way of being a good leader. Keep it in check and make sure you have people around you who you trust to tell you when the emperor has no clothes.

If you notice this behavior in the people you mentor, call them out on it and discuss why they act that way and what could be done to find other ways to motivate them. Recommend recognizing greatness in others not as a reflection of their own contribution but for that person's achievements alone. If they did have a part in that person finding success, help them to feel glad about that contribution and to remain silent about it. Let the other person shine. Most people will know who had a part in helping them, so there is no need to diminish the spotlight by calling it out. Teach them to shift the positive focus to others. They will then establish a reputation for being a selfless leader who lifts others up. That is someone others will want to follow.

Confidence is also displayed in how you react in both good and bad situations, but it lacks the toxic edge of arrogance. When something goes well, publicly praise those responsible and give credit to them. Do not look for anyone to acknowledge your contributions as a leader. That doesn't matter. If you make a mistake, be confident enough to admit it openly and to make it a teaching moment for others. Your well-placed and thoughtful confidence and decisiveness will inspire those traits in others. Your own assuredness encourages their confidence in you and in your ability to lead them well and bolsters their confidence in themselves. It will motivate them to take calculated risks, to be bold and innovative, to suggest unconventional approaches, and to surpass objectives.

Speaking of risks, the more risk you assume, the greater the results but the greater the possibility of failure as well. Be confident in your choices and think through the possible outcomes, including second- and third-order effects. Are those risks that can be supported should they come to fruition? Leaders who display good judgment, who are confident and decisive, and who don't wait for a perfect solution will have the support of their organization, from both above and below, even if they do not succeed on the first try.

You can doubt an idea, but don't doubt yourself. If an initiative fails, take another look at the idea and your assumptions. Did you miss something that should have been considered? Is the idea worthy of another try in a different way, or do you cut your losses and move on to something else? Ask yourself tough questions. Keep your poise and passion for it, but don't let that passion blind your judgment and objectivity. Most important, have the confidence in yourself to not tie your ego to your idea, and be ready to cut it loose if it is not the right solution.

If the results of a project turn out different from what you expected, that is fine. They could actually exceed expectations, breeding more confidence and motivation for success throughout the organization. Remember, success may be worth an initial failure, and the confidence you have in your desired end state and your team's abilities and commitment will help them overcome any failure. You will show that failure is not an end state; it is merely an obstacle in the journey. You will display the self-assurance to recognize the failure, analyze the causes, and chart a new course for success.

HUMILITY

Humility is important in leadership and goes hand in hand with confidence. On a personal level, confidence and humility will give you the strength to take constructive criticism to heart and improve. If your ego exceeds your ability to internalize that feedback, then you will not succeed as a leader.

Everyone has heard of or worked with the humble or servant leader, who always puts the organization and its people first, ahead of their own personal interests. They do it without fanfare or expectations of recognition. Some leaders play the "humble pie" game, demonstrating a false sense of humility. You know the type: always fishing for compliments or reassurances that they are excelling. Those folks are exhausting, and that behavior is as transparent and inauthentic as arrogance. That behavior is normally tied to low self-esteem as well. People will see through a vacuous attempt to portray an image, and there are few things more irritating than false humility.

Keep your accomplishments in perspective and spend more time giving credit to others. If you are smart, you don't have to tell people how smart you are; they figure that out pretty quickly for themselves. Genuine humility goes hand in hand with empathy for others, self-awareness of how you are perceived, and a continuous desire to learn. Stay humble and don't ever let your ego get in the way of your effectiveness.

BEWARE ENTITLEMENT

I have always felt that I am only entitled to two things on the job: fair treatment and fair pay for my work. Everything else related to your job and your sense of entitlement may be interesting, but it is not relevant to what you should expect. Plus, people may not be willing to challenge you on that sense of entitlement, resulting in ethical missteps, which can be career-stopping. As you move up in stature in an organization, without a solid sense of self-awareness and humility, you can easily imagine yourself as the smartest, most beautiful, funniest person in every room (cue mandatory nervous laughter from your employees). You aren't.

Promotions and new positions of higher authority come with perks, benefits, or additional compensation that is above and beyond what the average employee receives. This can breed a misplaced sense of entitlement in leaders who lack self-esteem or humility, which can then lead to misuse of their position, a lack of empathy, or in the most egregious cases, criminal conduct.

Marie Antoinette's famous but probably apocryphal quote, "Let them eat cake," illustrates entitlement. Regardless of the historical accuracy of the quote, it drives home the point about how leadership can become disconnected from the conditions of those they lead. This disconnect, where treatment at the top is vastly different from treatment at the bottom, can germinate in an organization. This presents a slippery slope for leaders who lack awareness of it. The situation can be exacerbated if people looking up in the organization aspire to have those same perks or more as part of their position, where the perks become the focal point rather than doing good work.

As a leader, you need to keep yourself in check and be willing to listen to those who help keep you grounded. Find a trusted person or people in the organization, a mentor, or a family member, friend, or spouse who can speak bluntly, and listen to them. Those people should feel free to operate in your close sphere, knowing that you want people around you who will speak truth to power without fear of marginalization or retribution.

Status symbols, rituals, and perks can often set the tone for this sense of entitlement and can shape behavior in the wrong direction. Make a conscious choice of whether perks will be a part of your company's culture that is shared and embraced as a positive or something that becomes discriminatory and divisive, widening a gap between the haves and the have-nots.

ETHICS

The self-reflection that is missing from most jerks is the crucial element to avoiding this pitfall yourself. Reflect on your words and actions and how they will be perceived by others. Words matter, so choose them carefully. As a senior leader in the organization, even your offhand comments can be taken as direction or requests to act. As they say, "Perception is reality." *Your* reality is not necessarily the same as the reality of those around you.

Be aware that what you say will drive employee behavior and can lead to ethical missteps if you are not clear in your direction and expectations. For example, if you make a comment about doing a project, but you intended the comment as a joke, your attentive employees may take you literally, even if the facetious project is not relevant to the organization or not in their job jar. The jerk will often then say later, "Why did they do that?"—oblivious or unconcerned about the fact that they were the cause of wasted time and effort. So don't be that jerk. Be careful in what you say and remember that your words matter.

Being ethical—doing something because it's the right thing to do rather than because it will get you something—is also crucial, but it can be a tricky business. There are no exact formulas and many gray areas in ethics. You need a strong moral compass and good judgment to make the best ethical decisions. Something could be legal but not ethical, so legality is not a good metric. To maintain a higher ethical standard at all times, you must be able to judge what that standard is for yourself.

If you deal with problems ethically, consistently, and honestly, your actions will teach your subordinates how to do the same, giving them the framework to make good ethical decisions even at the lowest levels of the organization. Set the standard, empower them, and hold them accountable for ethical missteps. True ethical leadership is rooted in character, integrity, and accountability for your choices. Ethical considerations should drive your leadership decisions and actions, and if you apply strong ethical values as a core tenet of your leadership, then others in your organization will have more trust in you and will follow your example. You will establish a reputation as a leader of principle.

CONFRONTING THE JERK

When we are stuck with a jerk boss, we often ask ourselves, "But what can I do? She is the boss!" or "I am afraid he will retaliate against me if I submit a formal complaint or challenge him." Those are indeed risks of confronting a jerk. But as a leader, it is your responsibility to try to stop this behavior and to shield those beneath you from its toxicity.

How to do that is a good discussion to have with your mentor and with someone who understands the structure of your organization and the channels for addressing the behavior of the jerk for corrective action. You should always try to tactfully address the behavior with the person themselves if you can. Sometimes, people think they are showing good leadership and don't realize they are actually being a jerk. They may be open to doing something to correct it themselves. In many cases, they don't care about your opinion or that you think they are being a jerk; they think they are effective because the boss loves them or because they achieve results. This kind of jerk doesn't care about—or even recognize—the kerfuffles, dysfunction, distrust, and demoralization they create among the team. In those cases where the jerk behavior is the surface tip of a character flaw iceberg, you need to find other ways to address the destructive behavior.

If the jerk's behavior is illegal or unethical, there are ways in almost every organization to lodge a formal complaint, which could be done anonymously. Submit the complaint. Normally, this will involve contacting the human resources department, the Office of Equal Opportunity, or the inspector general if you work for a government organization. Be specific and unemotional in what you report, keeping the complaint focused on the facts of the most egregious behavior.

If it is a leadership style issue—for example, they are not very friendly or communicative, but they have not done anything unethical or illegal—then your case is much harder. You don't need to agree with your boss's style. But the question remains, does it create a hostile or toxic work environment? If so, don't allow yourself or others to excuse the bad behavior. If there are others who have witnessed the behavior and can corroborate your claim, submit the complaint from the group. Then it cannot be written off as simply a "personality conflict."

Having bona fide facts and specifics will help your senior leadership and investigators look into the allegations to see if they are substantiated. Good organizations will indeed investigate these types of complaints, and will act on them when appropriate. If you work in an organization that does not pursue an investigation, you may want to consider whether you want to invest your time and talents there, given the obvious disconnect in values.

ANTILEADERSHIP

Sadly, there are lessons to be learned from the jerk about what *not* to do in a leadership position. I call them antileadership lessons. Pay attention to the jerk's methods and values, as well as their goals and what they do to achieve them, then avoid those like the plague. Imprint in your memory how it felt to work for someone like that and do everything you can to avoid creating that feeling in those you lead or mentor.

Antileadership takes a toll—mental, emotional, and physical—on the people who have to live through it. It can cause you to question your commitment to the larger organization because of leadership's inability to see the jerk's flaws or disinterest in a remedy. One jerk I worked for actually induced so much stress that it caused heart issues for me. The doctor had me wearing a monitor for a month so we could figure out what was going on and treat it. During that time, the jerk transferred to another command.

When the doctor read the results, he said, "I can't explain it, but halfway through your test, your heart jumped back to normal readings."

Oh, I could explain it.

Inventory a jerk's flaws and make a conscious effort to never repeat those behaviors, even under your most stressful circumstances. When working for a jerk, you learn to look beyond those who immediately report to you to see if you are missing the jerks beneath you—those a level below your direct reports who may be toxic. You learn to not make excuses for the jerk, and if they are not open to feedback (usually the case, because they lack self-awareness), then you try to shield those beneath you from the bad behavior so that you take the brunt of it on their behalf. Don't pass it along. Contain the chaos at your level.

Most of all, when working for a jerk, you learn how you will never, ever treat someone as a leader, and you use any means available to you in the organization to ensure that they are held accountable for their poor leadership choices. Five percent jerks in any organization is 5 percent too many. Don't accept it.

SEA STORY

ANTILEADERSHIP LESSONS FROM A JERK

I was in an operational job, a very high-stress position, the kind where you had to be constantly on your game, thinking two steps ahead to be prepared for anything. I was part of a core group of leaders in the organization who reported to the next person in the chain of command right beneath the commander. Most days, those of us in this senior leadership group interacted with this intermediate supervisor but not the big boss. Therein lay the problem: The intermediate supervisor was a jerk. He had grown up in a culture where bad behavior was routinely recognized and rewarded as strong leadership. He was used to people working horrendous hours, berating individuals publicly for perceived poor performance, and using threats and intimidation or callous

continued

treatment as a way to achieve results at any cost. Because the supervisor—like many jerks—got results and managed up very well, his worst behavior was hidden from the boss.

In the military, we know there will be times when we are called on to give more than 110 percent. A critical mission or crisis demands that, but it is not normal operations. However, there are leaders who do not understand how to operate in a measured, reasonable way; instead, they create crises to feel important, to divert attention from their shortcomings, or because they simply don't have any idea of what they should be doing. Just "doing something" looks like success to them. They lack the maturity to exercise good judgment and an understanding of what it means to truly lead people well with humility, purpose, and empathy. In any organization, the jerk does not instill loyalty or trust. That lack of trust becomes a critical leadership liability during times of crisis.

Our organization had been assigned to respond to an operational crisis, and the intermediate supervisor responded to the pressure as expected: He became more of a jerk. His menacing manner, meant to intimidate, only caused people to shake their heads in disbelief and to work around him to get the mission done.

While humor can be used by leaders in a positive manner, some like this jerk used demeaning, embarrassing "humor," the cheap shot, as a way to intimidate or belittle subordinates. His attempted "jokes" were not funny and were certainly inappropriate. Good leaders know the difference.

The irony here was that the jerk thought the success of the mission was due to his leadership (again, no self-awareness), but it was really attributed to the stellar leadership of the officers, chiefs, and sailors who persevered *despite* him, not *because* of him. He never understood that and probably doesn't to this day. But everyone in that organization learned how to get the mission done in his leadership void.

THREE POSITIVES

1. Leadership lessons can be learned in even the worst circumstances with the worst leaders.

2. Missions can be achieved by good people in the organization, even when there is a bad leader.

3. Most jerks don't stay in one job or position forever, so there is opportunity for an astute leader above them to discover the truth.

Good senior leadership should always have their antenna up for the jerk beneath them and take swift, decisive action to correct the jerk's behavior or remove them from the organization. True leaders will not let the situation persist and will report or directly deal with bad behavior. In most cases, the jerk's leadership deficiencies are character flaws that run deep and cannot be easily reformed, so reporting them and having them removed would be the best solution.

LET YOUR FREAK FLAG FLY

At the end of the day, your leadership and mentoring style is your own. You can get as much advice and counsel from others as you like. They will all have an opinion about what you should do and how you should act. Being a great leader and mentor means developing other strong change leaders and mentors. Hopefully, our conversation throughout this book has shown that in real-life situations, great leadership isn't rocket science if you just stay focused on what matters most. In fact, it's so easy a monkey could do it.

Recognize that you are tenacious, smart, bold, decisive, caring, innovative, and honest. Use those great qualities. You know what you need to do. Just do it and own the outcomes, good or bad. Be humble enough to admit mistakes and confident enough to not let obstacles deter you. Don't ever limit yourself or let those you mentor limit themselves. Put others before yourself and always look for a way to shine the light on the excellence of the team. Be genuine, demonstrate integrity, but most of all, just be yourself. Let your freak flag fly, and others will show up with their papier-mâché and tin foil hats to march with you in your parade.

ACKNOWLEDGMENTS

MY MENTOR MESH

I have had many great mentors over the years and would like to give some of them a shout-out and special thanks here. If I have missed anyone, please don't think it was intentional; it is purely oversight and regrettable, and dinner is on me next time we meet up.

Thank you to my amazing mentor mesh: Admiral Bill "Fox" Fallon, Monica Shephard, Sue Higgins, Admiral Mike Gilday, Admiral Jan Tighe, Admiral Matt Kohler, and Admiral Tim White, as well as Admiral Gretchen Herbert, Admiral Diane Webber, Admiral Jan Hamby, Admiral Nancy Brown, Admiral Kathy Creighton, Admiral Nancy Norton, Major General Maria Barrett, Admiral Paul Becker, Major General Jim Begley, Admiral Robin Braun, Major General Joe Brendler, Admiral Brian Brown, Admiral Carl Chebi, Major General John Davis, Admiral Sean Filipowski, Major General George Franz, Admiral Ron Fritzemeier, Admiral Dave Hahn, Admiral Sinc Harris, Admiral Betsy Hight, Admiral Jerry

Holland, Admiral Michelle Howard, Admiral Mary Jackson, Admiral Kevin Kovich, Lieutenant General Susan Lawrence, Admiral Kevin Lundy, Admiral Kelly Aeschbach, Lieutenant General Allan Lynn, Brigadier General Lorna Mahlock, Lieutenant General Kevin McLaughlin, Admiral Will Metts, General Paul Nakasone, Admiral Frank Pandolfe, Admiral Steve Parode, Admiral Gene Price, Lieutenant General Lori Reynolds, Admiral Kurt Rothenhaus, Admiral Bob Sharp, Lieutenant General Bob Shea, Admiral Dave Simpson, Major General Bob Skinner, Lieutenant General Vince Stewart, Admiral Nora Tyson, Lieutenant General Chris "Wedge" Weggeman, Major General Garrett Yee, Jim Adams, Mark Andress, Teri Bandur-Duvall, Peter Barnes, Claude Barron, Ken Bible, Diane Boettcher, Joe Boogren, Joyce Brocaglia, Tony Bruner, David Byrd, Rob Carey, Bobby Carmickle, Palvin Cebak, John Chandler, Jeff Cole, Norma Corrales, Ray Cross, Michael Dillon, Sarah Doherty, Kathy and Jim Donovan, Fred Eshleman, Dave Fischer, Boyd Fletcher, Jerry Flowers, Urs Foley, John Fristachi, Vic Gavin, John Gelinne, Carlton Griffin, Mark Guzzo, John Hearne, Sean Heritage, Manuel Hermosilla, Jeff Hesterman, Skip Hiser, Damen Hofheinz, Lee Johnson, Jon Kaltwasser, Mark Kosnik, Rick Ledgett, Mary Ann Lipinski, John "Gucci" Malfitano, Linda Maloney, Andrew Mansfield, Kathy Mayer, Cathy McCoil, Joel and Jackie McElhannon, Chris Miller, Scot Miller, James Mills, Terrance Mitchell, Ruth Morton, Mike Murphy, Don Owens, Chris Page, Terry Parham, Jim Price, Cecil Robinson, Toby Ruiz, Bennie Sanchez, Julie Schroeder, Frankie Shaw, Al Shockley, Gerry Slevin, Curtis "CJ" Smith, Reid Smith, John Stafford, Scott Starsman, Tina and Chan Swallow, Wayne Swan, Barry Tanner, Bob Tavares, Arthur Tulak, Tim Turk, Shawn Turskey, Delores Washburn, Dave Weddel, Lynn Wright, John Zangardi, and so many more. Thank you so much!

Special thanks to the outstanding photographers: Joe Lyman of LymanDVM Photography at https://www.facebook.com/Lyman-DVM and Hayley-Ann Vasco at https://hayleyannvasco.com.

And thank you to Allison Reynolds of Smithfield Horse and Carriage for letting us take a picture of her beautiful horse, Remington Steele.

EXPECTATIONS

H ere, you'll find an example of an expectations document that I provided my employees and the discussion of what I expected from each of them and what they could expect from me. The goal with this document is to give all of your reports, your new hires, and yourself a set of guidelines for everyone to follow. I gave this to my subordinates and discussed it openly and frankly with them so we could move forward with clear expectations and a common understanding of what mattered most.

WHAT I EXPECT OF YOU

Change is inevitable. I understand that change will be stressful, and we want to minimize that stress as much as possible and continue our mission. Instead of fearing change, embrace it and seek opportunities for the organization, your teammates, and yourself personally. Be flexible. Identify problems, gaps, and seams in the processes we have in place and make recommendations on how we can improve them. Don't wait for a command climate survey to provide feedback on how we can improve (either the work itself or the work environment). Provide feedback through your supervisor or the commander's electronic suggestion box if you wish to remain anonymous. Your supervisor and leadership team are here to help— so please give them the opportunity to address your concerns.

Tangible action

Ensure you are engaged with our customers and stakeholders and know whether we are exceeding their expectations. Identify where we are falling short and address that promptly and transparently. Always look for ways to ensure that what we are doing results in tangible actions and improvements at the end of the day. For example, having a meeting to build a PowerPoint brief to talk about the problem or solution is not a tangible action. Putting your specific plan in place with milestones and deadlines and tracking those actions until they are completed and institutionalized for the long term are tangible actions. Ensure an outcome, not output. Most of all, do not just admire the problem.

Coordination and collaboration

Coordination and collaboration are key to our success. Engage often and transparently with stakeholders, customers, and others who support our mission. Any time we can coordinate processes and identify solutions that will fix problems on a larger scale, I expect us to do that.

Always think of the situation in the context of the larger enterprise or environment, and put in place systemic fixes to problems we find.

Think in terms of aligning our actions with all of our stakeholders. You will need to ensure that your work and what you propose have the broadest stakeholder involvement to ensure success. I would rather us overinform folks than not have the right people clued in to what we are doing and participating in getting solutions out to the broader community.

Frank and honest discussion

You are the expert, and we rely on you for well-researched and -staffed recommendations. If I am making a bad decision, speak up so we can shift course. Suggest an alternative approach that you think would be better.

Keep leadership and your teammates informed—with both good and bad news. Good news is wonderful to receive, and we would like to ensure those good news stories get out quickly to recognize our superstars. Conversely, we also need to hear the bad news without delay. Bad news is like cheese: It won't get better with time. I expect bad news to be followed by how you recommend we move ahead to get a positive tangible result, how we learn from the issue or mistake, any follow-up, and any necessary administrative or disciplinary action. Failure is OK when you have thoughtfully considered all of the facts and contributing information but simply made a bad decision. We learn more from our failures than our successes sometimes, so analyze and act on what you learned.

When reporting information outside the organization, do so in accordance with whatever instruction applies and within the timelines required. Following through and keeping your leadership and teammates well informed are essential. We need to ensure we all stay aligned on leadership priorities, the messages, and the way ahead and that our decisions are informed by reality.

Continuous improvement

When presenting ideas and recommendations, present more than one option and be prepared to discuss the pros and cons of each and why you would pick one over the other. Remember, you are the expert; I am looking for your expert advice, so be bold and innovative. Always challenge conventional thinking and assumptions about the art of the possible. The preferred method for proposing these types of ideas is in an initial Word document of one page or less to be followed by other discussions as necessary. The format for this document is provided on the command portal.

Respect for and adherence to core values, standards, and instructions are paramount. Do not allow subordinates to cut corners. If there is a flaw in an order, instruction, or direction, let's identify a better alternative. We will then work to change or improve flaws through the proper channels.

Taking care of our people

Ensure that we are doing everything we can to prepare our personnel for advancement and promotion. Help them through difficult situations and recognize their outstanding work.

Be kind and positive. As Colin Powell says, "Optimism is a force multiplier."

I expect our senior leaders to all be mentors and role models for more junior personnel and to set the highest example through their actions. All personnel will have an individual development plan with specific actions and timelines in place that they have coordinated and discussed with their supervisor, and the supervisor will assist them in reaching those goals. Supervisors and employees will review those plans quarterly to ensure they remain on track and that the organization is helping to meet their professional growth and development needs.

Lead by example

I want to make sure we all lead by example and that subordinates understand what we expect of them at all times. (A lack of integrity, sexual harassment, racism, fraternization, substance abuse, etc., will not be tolerated.)

Know our personnel—their families, career goals, and any issues they may be having where we can help. People don't make monumentally bad decisions overnight. It is normally a gradual process of many small bad decisions that lead to a big one. Help course-correct those marginal behaviors before they escalate.

Lead by example in demonstrating work-life balance. No one should ever lose vacation days or feel that they cannot plan ahead and take time off. I do not want people to ever feel guilty for asking for leave to attend an important event, and we need to accommodate that whenever possible. There are times we will ask more of you and need you for longer hours, but that is not every day, so keep that work-life balance in check. Allow employees to take advantage of all programs that support a healthy work-life balance (command gym, telework, flexible work schedule, etc.).

Ensure new personnel are properly brought onboard and made to feel welcome as part of our team. Assign someone to help them navigate their first few days through the organization.

Ensure that our workforce is properly and promptly recognized with awards that we have the authority to give and that we are finding opportunities for them to receive training that will help them advance. Document and recognize outstanding performance quickly, publicly, and frequently. Be creative in how we reward folks.

Document substandard performance quickly with recommendations on how to improve. For documentation of substandard performance, ensure you work through the human resources office prior to issuing any documentation in writing. Follow through to make sure the person took corrective action and is meeting standards.

Work, think, and act as a team

I expect all of us to be more interested and invested in the team's success than in our own personal success. Be a person of your word: If you say you will do something, the team is depending on you to do it.

Budgets will be getting tighter in the coming years, so identify ways we can save money and be more creative in providing better service with the resources we have. Reward those who come up with improvements and creative solutions. Look for ways to conserve travel money (use web-based video teleconferencing whenever possible, share rental cars with other company personnel when on travel outside our geographic region, authorize only the minimum number of personnel required to travel to the same event, use command vehicles for day trips and send only the minimum number of personnel required, etc.).

If you are unclear about what is required from senior leadership, just ask. We want to make sure direction and guidance are clear so we do not have folks going off in the wrong direction wasting time and getting frustrated. If the priority of the task in relation to other tasks is unclear, ask.

The number of hours worked does not impress me; the quality of your work does. Focus on quality.

Paperwork should be properly staffed and checked for quality before it gets to your supervisor or senior leadership. Attention to detail will reduce rework. Ensure all references and coordination are done prior to submitting.

We owe our staff prompt responses to their requests. All special requests will be processed and an answer provided within twenty-four hours. If you cannot meet that deadline because you need additional time to coordinate the response, let the person know via email when you expect to have the answer back and why the delay.

WHAT YOU CAN EXPECT OF ME

I will provide you a safe, professional work environment where your work is valued and contributes to our important mission. You will be appropriately compensated for your work. I will ensure the workplace is free from discrimination, harassment, and toxic leadership.

I will recognize your outstanding contributions and will identify and work with you to correct shortcomings. I will provide opportunities for promotion and professional development. I will understand your personal goals and help you to achieve them.

I will listen to and support your ideas aligned to the company mission and objectives for excellence. I will communicate our vision, goals, values, objectives, and expectations clearly and frequently. I will communicate and collaborate with honesty, frankness, transparency, and inclusiveness. If there is a problem, I will communicate early and often what is happening so you are not surprised.

I will respond to your suggestions or concerns quickly and thoroughly. I will investigate any instances of misconduct in the organization.

What else can I do for you, and what else do you expect of me?

My leadership style preferences

I prefer face-to-face (in-person or web video) communication for sensitive or contentious conversations. If it is a crisis, please let the support staff know that you need to get in to see me urgently.

If I ask a yes-or-no question, provide the yes-or-no answer first, then you can get into all the gory details of why.

When scheduling meetings, if one of my appointments is running over, I will reconvene that next meeting. I don't want folks sitting around waiting on me. I will ensure that I have read all of the required materials for meetings and briefs with sufficient time to prepare.

Liaise with staff appropriately and maintain a positive, helpful demeanor. You represent me when speaking to people outside our organization. Be careful with saying, "The boss says." Only use that when you've actually heard me say it or read that I've said it.

Know the organizational ethics rules about what you can and can't do. I know you will want to do extra things to help me out and be kind, but I want to ensure that you keep to only what it is you are authorized to perform.

When I am on leave or traveling, send me a quick report at the end of each day containing any hot issues for my awareness.

Let me know if there are people that I should recognize in a "drive by"—a short note about what they did that was exceptional so I can stop by their cubicle and thank them. Remember, it doesn't take a lot to make someone feel special and appreciated.

BONUS SEA STORY– FOR THE DIEHARDS

ELEPHANTS IN THAILAND

Work-life balance applies equally across the board from those with families to those who may be single or not have children. The "life" balance can and should include hobbies and activities that keep you sane and happy. That could be anything: sports, quilting, reading, music, cooking, volunteering, gardening, hiking, photography, skydiving, adventure travel, competitive dog grooming, collecting navel fluff, attending the Renaissance Faire dressed as a faun satyr . . . whatever your interests. Make time for those breaks and show those who work for you that you are taking time to enjoy life outside work to recharge your life batteries.

I was on an exercise in Thailand several years ago. It was my first time in Thailand and I was in awe of the beauty of the landscape and people as we drove to our exercise location. Once there, we were working long hours on operations supporting the exercise, so basically, we were going from where we slept to where we worked every day. At the end of every military exercise, there is an event called the "Hot Wash," where leadership is briefed by the different team leads on lessons learned and what should be studied further in subsequent exercises—what went well, what didn't, and what could be done better next time. It is a useful drill to go through and is a standard post-exercise activity.

At the end of our exercise, our Army colonel (a great leader who I loved working for) stood up and said, "Hooah." (This is a word Army folks love to punctuate their discussions with, and it can mean anything from "great job" to "yes, sir" to a bunch of other meanings. For some it becomes a staple of their vocabulary that if taken away would leave them truly speechless.) He continued, "Great job on the exercise, hooah. Tomorrow is the Hot Wash and is mandatory for O-6 and above." For nonmilitary types, an O-6 is a senior officer, a Navy captain or an Air Force, Marine, or Army colonel. At the time, I was an O-5, a Navy commander, so I raised my hand and said, "Sir, so it is *not* mandatory for O-5 and below?" He looked a bit perplexed but replied, "Well, hooah, Commander Barrett, it is not but I would think you would want to attend for your professional development." To which I replied, "Well, hooah, yes, sir, thanks, but I am going to go ride elephants in Bangkok tomorrow." And, carpe diem, I did. I decided that I may never get back to Thailand again, and it was an opportunity I didn't want to miss.

Was there a measure of professional risk in not going to the Hot Wash? Sure there was. Could someone have interpreted that as my not being committed to the organization's mission or my professional development, and could it have been reflected in lower performance evaluation marks? Sure. Was I fairly confident that my leadership, peers, and

continued

subordinates knew I was a good, hard worker based on my past performance and committed to the organization, and would think this was fine in the end? Yes. Therefore, it was a risk I was willing to take. I also knew that I would be able to read all the after-action reports on the exercise to understand the lessons learned and what we needed to improve on for the next event. So, I and several others, including some more junior to me who may not have felt free to do the same until someone in their leadership sent the message that it was OK, saw an amazing piece of Thailand that we would have missed had we not seized the opportunity. In doing so, we achieved a balance—very hard work and a great life experience that I still reflect on to this day. I am a carpe diem kind of gal, so seeing Thailand was important, and years later, it is, frankly, the only thing I remember about the whole exercise—another great adventure I have the Navy, my colonel, and the great leadership at that organization to thank for. As they say, join the Navy and see the world . . . and we did.

THREE POSITIVES

1. Our leadership recognized that work-life balance and having a great adventure was important and supported us.

2. Perspective. If it won't matter three years from now, don't worry about it.

3. The elephants in Thailand were a wonder to behold, gentler and more intelligent than I could have imagined.

+++

ABOUT THE AUTHOR

FORMER REAR ADMIRAL DANELLE BARRETT is a mom, wife, daughter, sister, and friend. She was born in Buffalo, New York, and graduated from Boston University in 1989 with a bachelor of arts in history. She received her commission as an officer from the US Naval Reserve Officers Training Corps in a ceremony aboard the USS *Constitution*. She holds a master of arts in management, national security strategic studies, and human resources development, and she earned a master of science in information management.

As an admiral, Danelle served as director of current operations at US Cyber Command and as director of the Navy Cyber Security Division and deputy chief information officer on the Chief of Naval Operations staff. In her last position in the US Navy, she led the strategic development and execution of digital and cyber security efforts, enterprise information technology improvements, and cloud policy and governance for 700,000 personnel across a global network. An innovator, she implemented visionary digital transformation to modernize with unprecedented speed, significantly improving Navy Information Warfare capabilities. Her numerous operational assignments included deployments to Iraq, on an aircraft carrier in support of operations in Afghanistan, and to Haiti providing humanitarian assistance and disaster relief after the 2010 earthquake.

She currently executes a portfolio of work that includes being an independent director on several corporate boards, consulting, public speaking, and writing with more than thirty-five articles published. And most important, for fun, she signs up to be an extra in movies.